CRANES
IN ACTION

Larry Shapiro

MBI Publishing Company

First published in 2000 by MBI Publishing Company, 729 Prospect Avenue, PO Box 1, Osceola, WI 54020-0001 USA

MBI Publishing Company books are also available at discounts in bulk quantity for industrial or sales-promotional use. For details write to Special Sales Manager at Motorbooks International Wholesalers & Distributors, 729 Prospect Avenue, PO Box 1, Osceola, WI 54020-0001 USA.

Library of Congress Cataloging-in-Publication Data
Shapiro, Larry.
    Cranes in action / Larry Shapiro.
        p. cm. -- (Enthusiast color series)
    ISBN 0-7603-0780-6 (pbk. : alk. paper)
    1. Cranes, derricks, etc. I. Title. II. Series.
    TJ1363 .S466 2000
    621.8'7--dc21   99-050042

On the front cover: A vintage LS-108 Link-Belt 45-ton crawler crane is used to set concrete barriers in preparation for roadwork to expand a highway. This crane is an essential piece of equipment for concrete barrier work.

On the frontispiece: The Liebherr LTM 1160 all-terrain hydraulic truck crane has a feature that permits the operator's car to tilt upward. This provides a more operator-friendly environment when compared to the older-style cranes that required the operator to constantly work in an awkward position in relation to the controls.

On the title page: A building project in the heart of Manhattan requires careful consideration for placement of the cranes. Due to the close proximity of neighboring buildings on all sides of the construction site, three gantry cranes on pedestals have been erected to handle the job.

On the back cover: A Manitowoc Epic Series M250T lattice boom truck crane works at a city construction site setting precast panels for a new condominium building. The truck carrier has seven axles to support this massive crane. The crane has a lifting capacity of 300 tons and is owned by Central Contractors Service.

Edited by Paul Johnson
Designed by Dan Perry

Printed in China

CONTENTS

ACKNOWLEDGMENTS 6

INTRODUCTION 8

Chapter One   CRAWLER CRANES 11

Chapter Two   TRUCK CRANES 31

Chapter Three   TOWER CRANES 57

Chapter Four   AUXILIARY CRANES AND BOOM TRUCKS 67

Chapter Five   SPECIAL APPLICATION CRANES 85

INDEX 96

ACKNOWLEDGMENTS

It is amazing how often we can overlook the most obvious things until we decide to look for them. This was the case when I became interested in developing this book. I passed a construction site in downtown Chicago where a tall building had recently been torn down. The vacant lot was surrounded by large fences with plywood sides and an overhead platform to protect pedestrians from any falling debris from the new construction. The plywood walls surrounding the job site were painted with advertisements about the new building, and along with information about the available space was a drawing of the finished product. It was a gloomy day in early winter (one of just two seasons that we experience in Chicago, the other being road construction).

As I passed an open gate, I saw this enormous crawler crane fitted with an attachment that I had never seen or perhaps just not paid any attention to. When I asked about the job, I was told that I was looking at a caisson rig that was digging holes 100 to 200 feet below the surface that would eventually act as the main support base for the new building. I considered getting my camera from the car and then took into account the ugly day. Still, my desire to photograph this exciting operation won out.

On the way home, I suddenly realized that there were cranes everywhere. Tower cranes loomed over high-rise projects, all-terrain hydraulic truck cranes were setting precast concrete forms, crawlers were setting iron, and even the guy delivering garbage dumpsters was using a small crane. Almost every day since, no matter what city I have been in, I have seen an overwhelming number of cranes doing countless jobs. Some were new and others were old and rather beat-up looking. Each time I followed a stick on the horizon, I found bigger cranes making even more impressive picks.

At least 99.9 percent of crane operators were open to having pictures taken and conveyed pride in their work as they described the job and equipment. Only one incident was anything less than friendly and almost resulted in physical damage to my car and me. A lunatic foreman and his band of cronies chased after me and tried to prevent me from leaving a parking lot adjacent to their job site where I was photographing a crane.

Regardless of my misadventure, the individuals listed alphabetically here went out of their way to educate me through personal interviews and by supplying me with an abundance of literature and product specifications to produce this book. They have on occasion supplied me with information about interesting picks. I would never have been on the Dan Ryan expressway on Chicago's South Side at 2:00 in the morning to photograph a 500-ton Liebherr hydro if I hadn't received a heads-up beforehand. My thanks go out to: Vaughn Airy, Pioneer Cranes; Michael Larson, Manitowoc Cranes; Michael Lawson, Liebherr Cranes, Schiller International Corporation; John Martello, Central Crane Company; Mike Monohan, Central Crane Company; Ray Pitman, Pioneer Cranes; Kristine Poulson,

A crawler crane is fitted with a caisson drilling attachment to prepare the foundations for a downtown high-rise building. The bit is just descending into the hole to continue digging. Another crawler can be seen in the background preparing to place a steel column into a hole that will later be filled with concrete. The operator can be seen using mechanical levers to control the crane functions.

Anthony Crane Company; Mike Ricigliano, Anthony Crane Company; Mike Stevenson, Stevenson Crane Rental; and Ernie Vole, Jr., Ernie's Wrecker Service.

Those who love me the most have said that some of my interests have become borderline obsessions. It must be contagious, because during the research of this book, I received calls from my father, my sister Barbara, social clients, and commercial clients about interesting job sites with cranes that I might care to look into. People who had no interest in cranes at all would tell me that they passed the most incredible crane just the previous day.

To everyone who has been inadvertently bitten by my obsessions, thank you for your considerations.

In the previous books I've written, I've always made a point of mentioning the help, support, and love that I receive from my wife, Dorothy, during the development stages of the book. The preparation for this book was no different. On several occasions she too has called to inform me of the cranes that she came across during her daily commute. Beginning the conversation with ". . . I can't believe I'm calling you, but I just saw the most interesting crane working. . . ." I would like to take this opportunity to tell her that I love her, and thank her for putting up with me.

—Larry Shapiro

INTRODUCTION

Building construction, the growing expansion of the industrial sector, and the ongoing repair of our nation's infrastructure (largely known as road construction) are responsible for a significant rise in jobs and productivity. National indicators that measure the successes of our economy rely heavily on the construction sector as a gauge. As this area continues to grow, workers, raw material suppliers, and heavy equipment manufacturers prosper, which causes a ripple effect through the entire economy. One constant throughout this sector is the need for handling and lifting materials. Cranes of one style or another are present everywhere construction and renovation take place. Whether a task involves building a house or a skyscraper, repairing an old highway or building a new bridge, upgrading a manufacturing facility or replacing a rooftop HVAC unit, a crane will be on the site.

The largest and most noticeable cranes can be seen erecting high-rise buildings or lifting the heaviest loads, but even small jobs use some type of crane. Utility companies, sign companies, mechanics, towing companies, and material delivery companies are just a few of the businesses that require assistance with moving or lifting heavy objects.

Travel through almost any town or city and a variety of sticks will be visible above the horizon. *Stick* is the affectionate term for a crane within the industry. The majority are crawlers, or hydraulic all-terrain truck cranes, which are also referred to as hydros or pickers.

At the time of this writing, the demand for cranes in some markets far outstrips the supply, and crane manufacturers are enjoying healthy backlogs for machines. In Chicago, tower cranes aren't curently available for rental due to the large number of high-rise projects under way.

A 1960s-vintage Manitowoc 3900T Vicon series lattice boom truck crane works at an urban construction site. The contractor is adding several floors to an existing building. The crane is configured with 360 total feet of boom and is setting steel beams that were unloaded previously and stored on the roof.

A 90-ton Lima conventional truck crane picks a concrete panel off the transport truck for installation at this job site. Since the panels are shipped flat, the operator must make a two-line pick to raise the panels upright before setting them in place for Nationwide Erectors.

Another major demand nationally for multiple cranes is in the construction of sports arenas in cities such as Los Angeles, Milwaukee, and Baltimore. These require as many as a dozen heavy-lift cranes per job site. And, of course, the largest public works project of the 20th century is under way in Boston building the Central Artery, otherwise known as the "big dig." Perhaps as many as 100 cranes have been dedicated to this project for a multi-year period.

Tower cranes, crawler cranes, truck cranes, and boom trucks each have specific duties and qualifications to perform the various jobs that they handle. Crane operators and oilers work with many different tradespeople to successfully accomplish the tasks at hand. Whether it's a carpenter receiving a delivery of lumber to build a house or an ironworker setting beams, the work is done together. It has long been a tradition of the ironworkers to celebrate setting the final piece of iron on a large project. It is not uncommon for the last beam to be signed by the workers or painted in a manner to reflect some aspect of the job, the client, something that was memorable during the time frame of the project, or the location. If the framework of a job site has a pine tree and an American flag sitting on top, it represents a union job and the message of peace.

In the early part of this century, many ironworkers were injured or killed while walking the beams. Fortunately, through the effort of regulatory agencies, unions, and contractors, ironworkers now have a much safer working environment. Still, the men and women who walk the tall steel thrive on the adrenaline rush that is inherent in the work they do. They say ironworkers get the big bucks because of the risks involved in walking on the beams high above the others. This initial framework is a necessary part of any major project. It is with this in mind that one has to remember the inherent dangers present when performing any work that involves heavy machinery.

Sadly, in July of 1999, three ironworkers were tragically killed at a job site in Milwaukee, Wisconsin, while working high above the infield during a pick to set a section of the retractable dome for the new Miller Stadium. Among the memorials laid at the job site was a patch containing photos of the three workers and the single line that read "Build it for them." In keeping with that sentiment, this book is dedicated to them:

William DeGrave
Jerome Starr
Jeffrey Wischer

C H A P T E R 1

CRAWLER CRANES

One of the most popular and visible of all cranes is the crawler crane. The mainstay of the construction industry, the crawler crane is diesel powered and propels itself around a job site on two sets of iron tracks. This type of crane is recognizable by the lattice boom that extends upward from the upper body works. Crawlers are the mobile cranes that require the most time for assembly and remain on the job site the longest time.

As explained earlier, cranes are often called *sticks* by their operators. *Iron* is another industry reference for a crane. The *pick* refers to making a lift, and the *set* describes placing the load where it goes. Cable is also referred to as *wire rope*, and the operator's module is called the *seat*.

Big names in crawler cranes are the German makers Liebherr and Demag. American manufacturers are led by Manitowoc, and include Link-Belt, American, and Lima. Kobelco, another name in the industry, is Japanese.

Although many cranes are owned by contractors, the majority are rental stock from companies that specialize in providing crane operations to a second party. If a contractor cannot keep a crane working full time, the investment and subsequent maintenance are not cost-effective. Rental companies make the large investments in different types of machines to enable them to fulfill any request for lifting. It is not uncommon for specialized cranes to travel great distances from state to state between jobs to keep them working, because iron sitting in a rental yard is not bringing in any money.

Scheduling and logistics to move the iron from site to site require a significant amount of work and planning. This includes arranging for the appropriate number of trucks to carry the components, determining the travel time, and making sure the trucks arrive in the correct order for assembly. In addition, setup time must be accurately scheduled to ensure that the crane is ready to perform the pick on time as required.

The Crane Itself

Most cranes consist of two sets of tracks, the car body, housing or upperworks, gantry, mast, boom, and the sheave block at the tip of

A Manitowoc M-250 crane with Series-2 counterweights and a Maxer attachment places a 174,000-pound purge bin vessel. The unit is rigged with 280 feet of boom, is working at a 70-foot radius, and had to clear a height of 78 feet. *Manitowoc Cranes, Inc.*

A vintage LS-108 Link-Belt 45-ton crawler crane is used to set concrete barriers in preparation for roadwork to expand a highway during one of the two seasons that are experienced in the Midwest: winter and road construction.

the boom. The car body is a superstructure to connect the tracks and the housing. The housing is where the diesel engine, the hydraulic system, the winch drums with the cable, and the position for the operator and crane controls are located. The mast extends upward from the rear of the housing. The steel cables that originate at the ro-tating winch drums go up and over the mast to the boom. The lines between the mast and the boom are called the pendant lines. Sometimes there is an intermediate piece between the mast and the tip of the boom. If this is the case, then the pendant lines originate at this position and run to the boom.

Λ luffing jib attached to a Manitowoc 777 Epic series crane reaches up and over this parking garage to deliver materials to the workers on the top floor. The operator is in radio communication with the workers to direct the supplies to the proper place.

A Grove 150-ton crawler rigged with 180 feet of main boom and 50 feet of jib picks steel beams for the ironworkers who are assembling the framework for this office building. Unlike the newer cranes that are self-erecting, this crane required roughly six hours to set up and the services of an assist crane.

One of the cables at the tip of the boom is referred to as the load line and the other is the whip line. The load line runs off the tip of the main boom, while the whip line often runs through the tip of a boom extension, known as the jib section. The whip line is a single-part line that is able to move quickly, which makes it appear to whip around. The load line is a multipart line for extra lifting power. This line makes the heaviest lifts. At the end of the load line is a sheave block to connect the lifting cables to the load. The size of the sheave block determines how many times the cable can be parted. "Parting the line" describes the number of times the cable is run between the sheave block and the boom tip. Each time the cable turns to go in the opposite direction is counted as a part. The more parts to the line, the greater the load that can be lifted. Threading the cable to the tip is called reeving. At the end of the whip line is a hook ball, also known as a headache ball. This nickname is derived from the headache that results when someone bumps into it.

The boom consists of the butt section that originates from the housing, the boom extension sections, the boom top, and a jib if used. Some models require a transition section that originates at the diameter of the other sections and narrows to the diameter of a smaller top section. Each section of the boom is attached using steel pins. Boom sections for crawler cranes feature tubular or angular steel construction in a lattice framework.

Since crawler cranes can be assembled to extend varying lengths depending on the pick, booms come in sections. Boom extension sections come in 10-, 20-, and 40-foot lengths. Other reasons for the sectional design include the need to logistically transport the cranes to job sites. Cranes need to be disassembled for transport and assembled on the job site. Since most flatbed truck trailers are no longer than 46 feet, the 40-foot boom extension becomes easy to transport.

Unlike other crane styles that can alter the boom length by nesting telescoping sections, crawlers need to be built to specific lengths corresponding to each pick that will be performed. The lattice design saves on weight over a solid boom. The less the boom weighs, the greater the load that the crane can pick. The weight of a heavier boom would factor into the total lifting capacity of the crane since the boom is being lifted at the same time as the load, thereby reducing the total capacity. The diameter of boom sections differs by crane design, so some, but not all, are interchangeable. Once assembled, the

An American crawler crane is rigged with a wrecking ball to demolish an old bridge in order to clear the path for a new suspension bridge over the Chicago River.

The Manitowoc 3900 crawler preceded the newer 777 series crane. Here, a 3900 is used to place pre-forms during the construction of a high-rise building. After one floor cures, the form is slid out the side of the building and placed on the floor above to begin the process again of supporting the new work.

boom is lifted with hydraulic cylinders and the load is balanced by counterweights that are added to the backside of the housing. Counterweights sit in the counterweight tray.

A jib is an extension beyond the boom top for additional reach and maneuverability. Usually installed with an angled offset to the 0-degree line of the main boom, the jib allows loads to be placed deeper into a job site than is possible with a perfectly straight boom. The length of the jib varies by the job requirements and the capabilities of the crane. Jibs are attached to the tip of the boom top and have a steel strut called the

15

A crawler is set up with a drill rig attachment and a pile driver at this Southern California job site. A worker with a safety line has to climb up the shaft to realign the pile driver with the post that will be driven into the ground.

This Link-Belt LS-138H 75-ton crawler crane is set with 170 feet of main boom and 40 feet of jib. It was on site for roughly two months picking steel beams that formed the framework of this building.

jibs from 70 feet to 200 feet with main boom sections from 140 feet to 250 feet in length.

The operator controls the crane with a series of handles, levers, foot pedals, or—in the case of the newer electronically controlled cranes—joysticks. Generally, the foot pedals control the speed of the winch drum in addition to driving the crane with a gas pedal and brake. Levers are for turning the crane while driving, swinging the crane for picks, and to control boom up and down movements. The process of turning is achieved by braking with the track in the direction of the turn while the opposite track continues to move.

In addition to the operator, cranes with a capacity in excess of 20 tons generally require the assistance of an oiler. This lower limit on the use of an oiler can vary between local union guidelines and locations around the country. The oiler's duties involve maintaining the crane, which includes regularly checking all of the fluid levels and keeping the crane clean. The oiler may also be responsible for driving the counterweight truck to the job. Assisting the operator with moving the crane around the site either by driving or by giving directions for safety is often another responsibility of the oiler. An oiler is not trained as an operator, but may gain seat time under the operator's supervision as a means of training to move up to the position of operator. It is not uncommon for an oiler to earn half the hourly wage and benefits of an operator.

Capacities for conventional domestic crawler cranes range from 45 tons to the new 1,000-ton crane introduced by Manitowoc at the 1999 Con Expo national trade show in Las Vegas. German crawler cranes have rated capacities up to 2,000 tons. As the capacity increases, so does the size of the boom, the housing, and the base.

main strut that juts out at 90 degrees to guide the whip line and the controlling cables. Longer jibs require a longer main strut or the addition of a secondary jib strut. A jib with two struts is called a luffing jib and has larger jib boom sections than most conventional jibs. A luffing jib may consist of a butt section, one or more extension sections, and a top section, or just the butt and top sections, depending on the length and load. The longer the jib, the lower the total lifting capacity at the tip. The larger cranes can support luffing

When construction, or in this case, renovation takes place in a congested area without much access, the placement and operation of a crane can be difficult. During the construction of an addition to a hospital in the downtown area of Harrisburg, the capital of Pennsylvania, the operator had to make blind picks from both sides of his working area for each load. Picks were performed on a main street that was behind a small block of buildings, and the job site was on the far side of the main hospital building. The 777 Manitowoc 175-ton crawler was maxed out with 220 feet of main boom that supported roughly 195 feet of luffing jib to reach over the buildings. All crane direction was via radios.

Unlike other crane styles, the crawler cranes, with the exception of the new 1,000-ton unit, do not use external stabilizers for support. The counterweights in conjunction with the different boom and mast configurations keep the crane in balance. Lifting capacities in excess of 2,000 tons are available. Most often this is accomplished with specialized cranes and rigging that is not associated with the standard cranes that are on the road every day.

Transporting crawler cranes involves between 5 and 50 truckloads of equipment, depending on the crane and the end configuration that is required to perform the pick. A 230-ton Manitowoc 888 ships on 10 or 11 trucks, depending on the amount of counterweights. The 21000 Manitowoc ships on 29 trucks, and the Link-Belt LS-138 80-ton crane ships on just 3 trucks. Because of the width of most cranes, the crawler tracks, the counterweights, all of the boom sections and rigging are removed for transport.

Industry and government standards require that the capacity ratings for crawler cranes represent 75 percent of the actual tip load that they can lift at each radius and boom length. This was meant to maintain a safety margin with every pick. A crane's capacity chart, referred to simply as the chart, is a table from the manufacturer that indicates the maximum lifting abilities at various radii from the crane's center that have been measured with different lengths of boom. Some cranes have the same maximum rating but different charts based on the structural designs. It is then said that one crane has a better chart than the other.

When measuring the lifting capacity or determining the weight of a load, several items figure into the calculation in addition to the actual pick. The weight of the load blocks, hooks, weight ball, slings, hoist lines, and the sheaves

Because of space limitations on the job site, a tower configuration was needed to complete construction of this low-rise building. The total building height did not justify the expense of a tower crane, so the contractor ordered a Manitowoc 3900 crawler crane with a tower attachment. The crawler can move around the job site and can use the jib extension to place materials wherever they are needed.

A close-up view of a Manitowoc 2250 crawler crane with a Maxer attachment for heavy lifts. The Maxer is on a wheeled carrier that follows the crane housing when it swings. Dielco of Las Vegas owns the crane. *Manitowoc Cranes, Inc.*

beneath the boom point are considered part of the main boom load.

The Modern Crane Market

Each crane manufacturer has unique crane designs, product enhancements, and proprietary elements. All offer a range of cranes with different capacities, and most have available various capacity-enhancing devices to boost each crane's chart. Some use fixed iron rings as a base of operations while others suspend additional counterweights from the rear of the mast to provide for heavier lifts and greater reach.

The color scheme is one easily recognizable element that sets most companies apart. American uses a dark yellow/orange color for the housing with black boom sections. Liebherr paints their cranes a lighter yellow with a white band on the rear of the housing: Liebherr booms are yellow. Link-Belt cranes are red and gray with black boom sections, and Manitowoc cranes and booms are bright red. Any company that purchases a crane can, of course, request a paint job either to match other cranes or just to set them apart from the rest. When this is the case, all bets are off with regard to identifying each crane at a glance.

American offers 12 crawler cranes beginning with the model S229 (maximum capacity of 60 tons) to the model 11020 (maximum capacity of 450 tons). They offer maximum main boom lengths from 100 to 200 feet and jibs that span from 190 to 300 feet. American offers capacity-enhancing accessories that can form the work horse cranes, the ring horse cranes, the sky horse cranes, and the tower cranes.

The work horse cranes utilize accessories that hydraulically extend the counterweights rearward up to 12 feet to increase the base rating in excess of 25 percent for 150- to 240-foot boom extensions. American's ring horse cranes also use additional counterweights as part of the configuration to provide up to 360-ton capacities. When ring horse cranes are set up, a larger boom

is used as the main boom and the standard boom becomes the mast. The American sky horse cranes represent four models with 150 to 390 feet of main boom and maximum capacities from 142 to 342 tons at a 30-foot radius from the crane. The largest sky horse configuration is the model 11320 which provides 165 tons of lifting capacity with 160 feet of main boom, and a luffing jib that is 70 feet long.

The American tower attachments for the crawler cranes are self-erecting for the tower, boom, and jib. Four models are offered with a maximum tower of 250 feet, with 170 to 200 feet of available boom plus 60 to 80 feet of jib. Maximum capacity with the tower attachment is 100 tons. American also has pedestal cranes that mount onto a pedestal base for stationary or elevated operations.

Liebherr has six base crawler models. Beginning with the LR 1250 and ending with the LR 11200, the maximum capacities without any of the accessories range from 250 metric tons to 1,200 metric tons. Models in between are the LR 1400, LR 1550, LR 1650, and LR 1800. The digits in the model number after the initial "1" correspond to the maximum capacity of each crane in metric tons. Main boom lengths begin at 124 feet and extend as long as 226 feet with jibs from 70 to 164 feet.

Cranes by Liebherr are electronically controlled and computerized. Models beginning with the LR 1550 are also self-erecting. This means that they can be set up without the help and expense of an assist crane. The 1600 series crane features a modular boom system that allows boom sections to slide within one another for easy transport. The LR 1800 is the most powerful standard crane. It features a modular design for disassembly and transportation between job sites and for ease of adaptation for each unique job. The LR 11200 is the world's highest crawler crane. All of the Liebherr LR series cranes have load-capacity-increasing derrick systems that feature either a suspended ballast

A Manitowoc 888 crane owned by Anthony Crane Rental is rigged with a ringer base and 300 feet of boom. The pick is a fin-fan unit at a Texas petrochemical project with a 332,244-pound load including the rigging. The boom height is 130 feet and the crane is working at an 85-foot radius. *Manitowoc Cranes, Inc.*

or a ballast trailer on wheels behind the crane. Although crawler cranes are generally for long-term on-site operations, under certain circumstances they are assembled for a single pick. Some job sites require the crane to work in extremely tight areas, which can present a problem finding enough space to assemble the long boom for a crawler crane. In most cases, a large hydraulic all-terrain (AT) crane on a carrier with wheels will handle the job. Liebherr offers another solution to this scenario, especially where the tight confines of the job site would prevent the AT crane from utilizing the outrigger stabilizers. Liebherr has the model LTR 1800, which is an 800-metric-ton hydraulic telescoping crane on crawler tracks. Just like the lattice boom crawler cranes, the crawler tracks provide superior stability and weight distribution over an AT crane with rubber tires. This allows the boom to telescope in and out to overcome a tight area without sacrificing the capabilities of a crawler to move around the job site.

Link-Belt currently offers six crawler cranes. The first two have the same 80-ton capacity while the others can lift 100, 150, 200, and 250 tons. These are the LS-series models 138H, 208H, 218H, 238H, 248H, and 278H respectively. Maximum boom lengths go from 150 feet to 330 feet of main boom plus 40 feet to 100 feet of additional jib length depending on the specific models. The LS-248H is currently the only model with an available luffing jib that can pick 42.5 tons when configured with 180 feet of luffing boom, 160 feet of luffing jib, and 30 feet of fixed jib.

Manitowoc has two different crane series, the Vicon and the newer Epic. The Vicon series consists of nine models and capacities ranging from 70 tons to 350 tons with maximum boom lengths of 210 feet to 310 feet. The Epic series offers 11 cranes ranging in maximum capacities from 80 tons to 831 tons as standard.

The Vicon series includes the 3900, 3950, 4100, and 4600 cranes with 100-, 150-, 200-, and 240-ton capacities respectively. These cranes

A Liebherr LR1550 700-ton crawler crane works to steady a tower in Burns Harbor, Indiana. The crane has a Superlift on the back, 200 feet of main boom, and 100 feet of jib using an SDWB boom configuration. It took 46 truckloads to transport the crane from Haverhill, Ohio, to handle this job. The tail crane is a Manitowoc 888.

One of the cranes being used at the Orlando International Airport to build the new multi-level parking lot is this Manitowoc 4100 crawler crane with a tower attachment.

feature mechanical controls. The Epic (Electronically Processed Independent Control) series includes the 111, 222, 777, 888, 2250, and 21000 cranes with 80-, 100-, 170-, 217-, 275-, and 831-ton capacities. Beginning with the 777 model and excluding the 21000, the Epic models can have capacities that increase slightly depending

on the counterweights installed on each unit. The counterweight configurations are referred to as different series: Series 1, Series 2, and Series 3. The Series 2 capacities increase to 176, 230, and 300 tons respectively.

These cranes are computerized and feature electronic controls. The mechanical levers have been replaced with joystick controllers for the boom operations and movement of the crane. Up to seven different joystick controllers are used to operate the crane. In the case of the 21000 model, even the traditional foot pedal functions are handled by joystick controllers. The ability of the operator to tilt the cab backwards for more comfort and better visibility during picks is also a feature of the Epic series cranes.

Unlike the other models, the new 21000 rides on eight crawler tracks. One of Manitowoc's design characteristics of the 21000 includes the ability to have two different positions for the crawler tracks. The narrow stance setting, which mounts the crawler frames directly to the car body, has an overall width of just over 9 meters and requires the use of outriggers to enable a 360-degree swing with any rated load. The wide stance extends the width to 14.5 meters with the use of a pair of steel beams to attach the crawler frames to the car body, in order to avoid the need for outriggers.

Manitowoc also offers capacity-enhancing accessories to increase the maximum lifting capacities for many of the crane models. These capacity-enhancing accessories include the MAX-ER attachments and ringers. The MAX-ER attachment is a counterweight unit that rests on wheels behind the crane. This counterweight unit is suspended from the mast and rotates or swings with the crane. With the MAX-ER attachments, lifting capacities can reach as high as 1,000 tons for the model 21000 that has a base crane capacity of 831 tons. The total lifting capabilities of the other models that use the MAX-ER jump from 200 tons to 300 tons, 230 tons to 661 tons, and from 300 tons to 500 tons.

This small crawler is fitted with a clamshell bucket to demolish an older building and make way for the renovation of a city neighborhood. Unlike the newer, electronic cranes, this unit has foot pedals and mechanical levers for the operator.

A ringer, another Manitowoc capacity-enhancing attachment, is a stationary platform base that supports the crane and allows for more counterweights to support an increased capacity for the basic crane. The result is that heavier loads can be lifted higher and at greater radii. Ringers are only available for specific models. One advantage of ringer attachments is the ability to have a smaller base crane that can be used often and still be able to increase the lifting capacity without having to own heavier iron that might not leave the yard quite as much. Also, due to the size of the base crane, ringers can be assembled in many places larger cranes cannot access. Some examples include placement on a barge, on top of certain building structures, and in highly congested areas.

The procedures for installing a ringer are as follows: At the onset, a dirt contractor needs to build a very compacted and level base. Next, truckloads of heavy timber mats are brought in and laid out where the ring will sit. Most often, the wood will be Douglas fir, and some sections are connected with steel rods. An engineer will "shoot the transit" to check level before a second layer is placed in the opposite direction over the first layer. An assist crane, along the lines of a 175-ton hydraulic all-terrain crane, will be on site to set the car body, tracks, upper body, and mast onto the platform. The assembly of the iron ring onto the platform follows this. It is secured in place with large screw jacks. High-strength beams connect the ring to the base crane, and large iron rollers are then set between the ring and the house. Next, the boom is pinned together and the counterweights, mast extension, and rigging are added. Some ringers can be assembled in as little as two to three days. The house rotates around the ring with 360 degrees of maneuverability. Ring bases vary in diameter from 36 feet to over 66 feet. The main boom of a ringer rests on and travels around the ring. This effectively moves the load stress forward and off of the basic crane. The main boom of the base crane becomes the fixed mast for the ringer and provides a higher point for the control of the main ringer boom. The ringer attachments include a back mast that gives extra support to the fixed mast, which in turn allows for additional lifting capacity. A 200-ton crane becomes a 450-ton crane when it is ringed, and a 230-ton 888 becomes a 661-ton ringer. Manitowoc also has a model M 1200 ringer assembly for the M-250 crane that tops out at 1,433 tons for the main boom capacity and 882 tons with a jib. Manitowoc claims better charts compared to larger cranes with similar capacities.

Mannesmann Dematic Corporation—Demag has ten different lattice boom crawler cranes ranging from 300 tons to 2,000 tons with the addition of capacity-enhancing attachments. The model numbers are CC1800, CC2500, CC2800, CC4800, CC6400, CC8200, and CC12600, and they are 300-, 450-, 600-, 800-, 1,000-, and 1,600-ton capacity units respectively. Each has electronic controls, cabs that tilt for better vision of the pick, and optional self-erecting capabilities. Demag provides equipment to enhance the capacities of each crane beginning with the CC2500. Their Superlift attachment consists of a central ballast unit on a carrier with wheels that rides behind the housing. Demag also has the Ringlift, which is a ring-type attachment that allows even load distribution on the ground. It can be used in conjunction with a Superlift to increase the base crane's capacity several times. If the need exists and the space is available, a crane and ring can also be moved around a job site on the crawler undercarriage.

Crane Assembly

Many older model, and several current model crawler cranes require a hydraulic crane to assist with the assembly of the crawler. Referred

A Manitowoc Vicon series 4100 crane was fitted with a ringer to make this heavy pick of a bridge support. Two supports were transported on a barge because of their size and were said to be the largest suspension bridge arches set in the Midwest. The second arch rests on a barge below.

to as an assist crane, the hydro is an added expense in both iron and the additional operator and oiler.

The assist crane is used to unload all of the crawler components and then align them around the upper works while workers make the necessary connections. As the transport trucks arrive

26

Chellino Crane Service is lifting a 127-ton heat exchanger at a chemical plant in Illinois. The crane is a Manitowoc 888 with a ringer working with 300 feet of boom at a 127-foot radius. *Manitowoc Cranes, Inc.*

ball. Older series cranes require more setup and teardown time than the newer cranes.

New cranes are self-erecting, which means they have been designed so that they can be assembled without an assist crane. This process still uses removable crawler tracks that are transported by truck. Each crawler requires a separate truck. The car body and the housing travel as a unit on another truck. Upon arrival at the job site, a self-erecting crane is raised off the truck bed by four hydraulic jacks that are part of the crane. They extend to the ground on either side of the trailer. After the unit is elevated, the trailer is driven out from under the crane. Next, the mast, with wire rope attached, lifts one crawler at a time off the transport truck and aligns it to the proper position. Workers make the necessary connections and the process is repeated with the other crawler.

The hydraulic jacks are then retracted, allowing the crane to rest on the crawlers. Now, using the mast again, the butt section is picked from a trailer, aligned into place, and pinned. Following this, the mast sets the stackable counterweights onto the counterweight tray, connects this unit with the gantry, and sets it in place on the rear of the housing. The remaining boom sections are lifted from the trailers and set into place and pinned before the cable is reeved. The crane can now pick the sheave block off a trailer to complete the installation. Some of these units can be assembled with as few as three people in a period of less than 12 hours. This labor and time saving improvement has inspired the purchase of many of the newer series cranes around the country.

Smaller crawlers, generally with capacities under 80 tons, transport on about five trucks and go together quicker than the larger cranes with longer booms and more complex rigging. While the newest crawlers can be assembled in just over 12 hours, more complex configurations can require a week or longer with one or more assist cranes.

The maiden pick by Manitowoc's first 21000 crawler crane was made in a chemical plant on the gulf coast of Texas. The crane is owned by Anthony Crane Rental and is rigged with 280 feet of boom while working at a 45-foot radius. It is setting up a 385-ton, 203 foot tall, 14-foot diameter distillation column. The configuration is for the base crane without the capacity enhancing MAX-ER attachment.

with the pieces that are needed, they must be staged and unloaded in the order in which the equipment is needed. The first step involves picking the housing off a trailer, followed by the crawler tracks. Next the boom sections are laid out and pinned together, followed by the assembly and hanging of the counterweights. Workers then run the wire rope through the boom sections to the tip and rig the sheave block or headache

On-site Job Duties

Crawler cranes are utilized primarily at job sites where a crane will be required for a period of weeks or months. Since crawlers can successfully navigate the poor ground conditions of many construction sites, they are ideal for mobility around the site. They also have the ability to pick and carry loads on the site. Crawlers do not require the use of outriggers like all-terrain truck cranes do, which enables crawlers to work in tighter quarters. Routine picks include precast concrete panels, forms for pouring concrete, lumber deliveries, and steel beams. Basic jobs that allow the crane to set up near the building will use a straight main boom, while jobs requiring more reach will necessitate the addition of a jib. The heavier loads with longer reaches will demand the use of a luffing jib.

If space constraints prevent the main boom from having the minimal 85-degree working angle, tower attachments with a jib will be fitted to the crane. This allows the crane to set up immediately adjacent to the building with a 90-degree rise straight up in the air. Tower attachments can reach tip heights up to 500 feet. The main boom and jib on a tower attachment are called the working boom. The newer cranes that do not offer tower attachments use luffing jib attachments for added reach. When a job site shuts down for the night with a working boom in operation, the boom is rotated over the backside until it folds down alongside the tower's mast. The tip is latched to the tower to eliminate any possible dangers from high winds. Tower setups are for light lifts that often represent the delivery of supplies and concrete to the upper areas of the work site. The crane's lifting capabilities are greatly reduced with this configuration.

The bigger crawler cranes are also used regularly for specialty jobs that may require several days of set up and tear down to perform a single pick. Chemical plants, refineries, and power plants are common job sites for extremely heavy picks. Regardless of the brand of crane, the available capacity-enhancement accessories are used to boost the lifting capabilities and the reach. Luffing jibs can provide tip heights up to 630 feet with 300 feet of jib boom. Ring-type attachments can offer up to 500 feet of tip height and capacities in excess of 1,400 tons at specified distances.

When a secondary crane is on site with a primary crane, it is either acting as an assist crane or a tail crane. As explained earlier, the assist crane helps to build the primary crane during the setup and teardown. The tail crane acts as a secondary crane during specialized picks or lifts that require two cranes. An example would be the setting of a large tank that is shipped to the job site on its side but needs to be set in a vertical position. The main crane will pick from the top of the tank while the tail crane will be rigged at the base. Both will lift the tank from the transport trailer and suspend it in the air. At a predetermined point, the tail crane will stop lifting while the primary crane continues until the tank is upright. The tail crane lets out some cable until the tank hangs free, and then the lines from the tail crane are released. The primary crane carries out the rest of the procedure alone.

Crawlers can pick and carry, which means that after the load is on the lines, the crawler can travel with the load to the position where it is to be set. A crawler's top speed averages between one and two miles per hour.

C H A P T E R   2

TRUCK CRANES

A lattice boom or conventional truck crane has the same boom characteristics as the lattice boom crawler cranes but uses a truck carrier with rubber tires instead of the crawler tracks. One advantage of the truck carrier is the addition of outrigger stabilizers. This gives a crane mounted on a truck carrier a greater capacity than the same crane mounted on crawlers. Whereas crawlers are rated at 75 percent of actual tested capacity, truck cranes are rated at 85 percent. The truck carrier also permits the main housing of the crane to be driven between job sites without having to be loaded onto a lowboy trailer. The boom sections, counterweights, and rigging still have to be trucked to the site on flatbed trailers.

The conventional truck crane most often handles jobs with a shorter time span than jobs requiring crawlers because the setup time is less. When compared to a telescoping hydraulic truck crane, the lattice boom units have a better chart at longer radii because of the weight savings that are inherent in the boom design. At short radii, lattice and hydro truck cranes with the same ratings have equal lifting abilities, although the lattice crane is quicker. A hydro crane requires more time to circulate the hydraulic fluid and extend or retract the boom sections. In essence, rotation, extension, and cable pulling are quicker with a conventional crane than with a hydro.

Another trait shared between lattice truck cranes and hydro cranes is the use of outriggers to stabilize the crane during operations. Both types use the same or similar truck carriers with all-terrain capabilities. As a matter of fact, the boom sections on some truck cranes can be interchanged between the use of lattice or telescoping hydro booms.

Companies that build conventional truck cranes include American, Demag, Grove, Liebherr, Lima, Link-Belt, Manitowoc, and P&H. The conventional truck crane market is the smallest segment compared to crawlers and hydros.

The Crane Market

American has several truck cranes available with maximum capacities from 75 to 300 tons. Main boom lengths can extend up to 290 feet along with jibs that combine with the main booms to permit a reach as far as 330 feet. Two of the truck cranes can be fitted with tower attachments that extend 250 feet at 90 degrees. These

This 75-ton Lima 700 TC conventional truck crane uses a steel bar suspended by a second line to keep the panel flat and prevent it from swaying. This saves damage and allows the panel to safely be slipped into place.

A 1995 300-ton Manitowoc M250T conventional truck crane works at a job site setting precast panels. The crane is working with 180 feet of main boom. The seven-axle crane requires a two-day setup and travels to the site via 11 truckloads. It is capable of decking its own house. The hydraulic cylinders raise the house off the flatbed trailer used for transport. After the trailer moves out, the carrier backs in and the house is lowered into place. This crane was on site for roughly four months. A 20-ton hydro truck crane was used to assist with the counterweights and boom sections.

can have up to 170 feet of boom plus 60 feet of jib attached to the tower.

Demag truck cranes are offered in 300-, 450-, and 600-ton capacities. They ride on carriers with seven or more axles and can be assembled in a variety of configurations for different lifts with the use of a light or heavy main boom. Cranes are offered with other options such as a fixed fly jib, a luffing jib, or Demag's Superlift rigging, which includes the use of additional counterweights that are suspended from the mast.

Liebherr has only one mobile crane with a lattice boom. It rides on an eight-axle truck carrier. The model LG 1550 has a rating for 550 tons with a maximum lifting capacity of 700 tons when configured for heavy lifting. It can handle boom lengths from 69 to 344 feet. In addition to the main boom, jib extensions are available from 69 to 299 feet for a maximum tip height of 541 feet. The crane, with its lattice boom (S), can be erected in many different configurations including the addition of luffing jibs (W), derrick booms (D), suspended counterweights (B), or a combination of each (SDWB) to accomplish the maximum capacities and reach. The lattice boom sections can be stored for transport by nesting them within other, larger sections.

Link-Belt offers three models, the HC-238H, HC-248H, and the HC-278H. These units have capacities of 150, 200, and 300 tons and can be configured with basic boom lengths of 50 or 60 feet. The maximum boom lengths are 240, 280, and 330 feet respectively. With slightly less than the maximum available booms, these cranes can have jib extensions of 70 or 100 feet, depending on the model. These units can also be configured with luffing jibs that enable them to lift up to 42.5 tons.

Manitowoc currently has two conventional truck cranes, the 777T and the M-250T. These are both part of the electronically controlled Epic series with base ratings of 220 and 300 tons respectively. Both models can handle 200 feet of main boom plus jib configurations with 30, 40, 80, or 120 feet depending on the model and the

While most truck cranes use H-style out and down stabilizers, this Lorain conventional truck crane has hydraulic outriggers of a different design. The crane is setting steel beams to top off a suburban office building.

amount of main boom. The 777T is the same as the 777 crawler with the exception that the 777T is on a five-axle rubber tire carrier. The 777T is rated at 220 tons compared to the 777's 150-ton rating. Like the crawler, the 777T features self-assembly and disassembly.

Depending on the size of the unit, the truck carriers will have between four and nine axles and will require special permits for road travel. Companies that install precast concrete panels like the truck cranes because of their speed. The panels are often shipped flat and have to be up-righted for placement. This can be accomplished with one crane using two lines in a maneuver called a tilt-up.

The primary line picks up the top of the panel while the secondary line picks up the base. Once the panel has cleared the truck that transported it to the job site, the secondary cable lowers the bottom while the top is raised. When the panel is in a vertical position, the bottom cable is released, allowing the panel to be set in place. The crane requirements for these jobs have increased over the years as the panels have gotten heavier. A panel that used to weigh 50,000 pounds weighs closer to 180,000 pounds today.

Hydro Truck Cranes

Cranes on wheels that have a solid, telescopic boom design are called mobile hydraulic cranes. This category encompasses several different crane styles including industrial cranes, rough-terrain cranes, truck-mounted cranes, and all-terrain cranes. All of these designs ride on rubber tires, though all are not road worthy. The range of lifting capacities for these crane styles ranges from 2 to 1,000 tons.

Hydraulic cranes are able to pick and carry, which means they can lift a load and then travel a short distance with it. The largest producers of

A Link-Belt truck crane on a four-axle carrier is the unit of choice to set the precast panels for this building.

Rigged with a full main boom and a jib, this conventional truck crane is setting the decorative top section for this low-rise office building.

Little Giant is a company that produces a small number of conventional truck cranes. This unit on a three-axle carrier is fitted with a clamshell bucket. Workers are widening a drainage canal to accommodate the runoff from the San Bernardino Mountains.

these crane types are found in the United States and Germany. The companies are Grove, Link-Belt, Lorain, and P&H in the United States, and Demag and Liebherr in Germany. Krupp, formerly a German producer of cranes, was acquired by Grove in 1995. The Japanese company Tadano also builds mobile hydraulic cranes.

Industrial Cranes

Industrial cranes are the smallest cranes overall in the mobile hydraulic crane category. These units are widely used for plant maintenance and small material-handling jobs. They are also called carry-deck cranes since the front of each unit has a flat deck that is meant to accommodate a load while the crane moves. One example is a crane with a 30,000-pound lifting capacity that has a deck-carrying capacity of 20,000 pounds. These cranes do not conform to federal requirements for vehicles that are allowed to travel on public roads. Industrial cranes can maneuver in tight quarters with both the front and rear axles able to steer. The operator's position is not usually in a fully enclosed compartment, just an open seat. Depending on the size of the unit, stabilizing jacks are optional.

This photograph's perspective is similar to the operator's view. Precast panels are set with a Manitowoc M250T conventional truck crane. This unit is owned by the Central Crane Company

A 1997 Liebherr LTM 1160-2 200-ton all-terrain hydro truck crane picks Spancrete concrete flooring panels and sets them into place at a condominium building project. The 200-ton unit was needed to accommodate the reach that was required throughout the site. The job was accomplished without the use of the lattice jib.

Lifting capacities range from 2 to 35 tons with maximum main boom lengths from 15 feet to 60 feet. These cranes also can accommodate jib extensions with from 7 to 20 feet lengths depending on the specific model. Depending on whether the cranes will be used inside or out, they are available with diesel engines for outdoor work or dual fuel (LPG/gasoline) engines for use inside. Broderson, Grove, and Shuttlelift are some of the companies that manufacture the industrial carry-deck cranes.

Rough-Terrain Cranes

Rough-terrain (RT) cranes, also called pickers, are not built to travel on public roads. These cranes are transported between job sites on drop deck lowboy trailers. They are designed to work on either solid ground or rough, uneven ground.

RT cranes are built with four-wheel independent suspension, have a compact design, and feature multiple steering modes for added maneuverability. The steering options include front only, rear only, crab (front and rear turn the same direction), and coordinated (front and rear turn in opposite directions). RT cranes utilize outriggers to stabilize the units during lifts. RT cranes have capacities ranging from 14 to 100 tons with main boom lengths from 60 feet to 114 feet. They are most often used for construction sites, bridgework, and as assist cranes.

Grove builds the RT cranes that are seen in the United States more than any others. They have 13 models with capacities ranging from 14 tons to 100 tons. These all have four wheels and are powered by 130- to 250-horsepower engines. Maximum boom lengths begin at 70 feet and extend as long as 125 feet. They can reach from 85 to 208 feet high. The larger units have swing-away jib sections to provide additional reach. These jibs can have a fixed length or be capable of telescoping for additional length. They can be

A Grove RT880 rough-terrain crane is working at a tunneling project site. The iron car with wheels travels on a rail within the tunnel to haul clay that is being removed. Here, after being removed fully loaded from the tunnel, it will be dumped and then lowered back into the hole for another load.

offset at 2-degree or 30-degree angles. All Grove RT cranes have enclosed cabs for the operators and are yellow.

Link-Belt currently has nine RT cranes ranging from 18- to 70-ton capacities. Top travel speeds are from 20 to 26 miles per hour under the power of various Cummins diesel engines. Maximum boom lengths range from 70 to 127 feet respectively. Each unit has a detachable lattice jib that can add between 25 and 67 feet of offsettable length in either fixed, two-piece, or telescoping sections. Link-Belt RT cranes are red and gray.

Tadano has 35-, 50-, 60-, and 65-ton RT cranes. Each has an enclosed operator's cab, multiple steering modes, and four-wheel drive. Tadano RT cranes have orange upper body works, black lower bodies, and white booms.

Truck-Mounted Cranes

The smallest truck cranes are 20 tons and affectionately referred to by many in the industry as taxicab cranes. These units typically travel to several short-term job sites in a day handling various quick picks. They can travel at highway speeds, albeit in the right-hand lane. These are not suited for rough-terrain sites and generally require solid ground beneath the wheels. Like all cranes, they are billed portal-to-portal, by the hour, and earn their money by being kept busy. Unloading machinery, transporting supplies to the roof of a construction site, setting steel, or placing an HVAC unit topside are common short-term jobs handled by truck cranes. The industry standard for these cranes is a four-hour minimum billing, portal-to-portal, for the 20-ton series cranes. Generally, the minimum billing increases to eight hours for cranes with capacities greater than 20 tons.

continued on page 45

A Lorain LRT434 rough-terrain crane is set up at another area where underground tunneling is being performed. The rail cars for removing dirt and clay are sitting next to the hole while the workers take a lunch break.

41

This P&H 50-ton rough-terrain crane is owned and operated by Anthony Crane Rental, Inc. It is working at an urban job site that does not require the rough-terrain characteristics of the crane. In order to provide the proper level base for the crane, the stabilizers in the street have been built up with the use of several layers of heavy timber. The stabilizer pads on the sidewalk are resting on round wooden boards to protect the concrete from damage.

A small Grove truck crane that is often used for several jobs in a day is unloading lumber supplies at a residential construction site. The truck carrier has three axles and five outriggers to stabilize the crane during lifting. Two are on either side and the fifth is at the front of the carrier. Heavy lumber is used under the pads of each outrigger to ensure a solid base.

Continued from page 41

These units are built to travel under their own power between job sites, driven by the operator. Depending on the size of the units, many have a capacity that is beneath the union base figure to require an oiler. Truck cranes set up quickly, feature a long reach, and have capacities ranging from 40 to 150 tons. These units feature swing-away jib sections that mount to the base section of the telescoping boom. Most often, the jibs feature a lattice design to reduce the overall weight and swing into position at the end of the top section, which is also known as the fly section.

The jib is affixed to the fly section with a set of steel pins and can be set at a 0-degree angle (which is in a straight line with the main boom), or at an offset of 15, 30, or 45 degrees. Similar in principle to the jibs affixed to crawlers or lattice boom truck cranes, the jib serves as an extension to the main boom for sheer distance or for reach over a building or other obstacle when used with the offset.

The TC offerings from Grove include eight models ranging from 40 to 150 tons of lifting capacity. Standard boom lengths begin at 90 feet and are offered as long as 173 feet with maximum tip heights of 152 to 270 feet respectively. These cranes ride on truck carriers with three, four, or six axles, depending on the model. The larger cranes, with capacities of 100 tons and greater, each have separate engines for powering the carrier and the crane. This entire line of cranes has two outriggers on either side in addition to a front downrigger to stabilize the unit during lifts.

Link-Belt currently has five truck crane models capable of picking from 40 to 100 tons. Travel speeds range from 56 to 60 miles per hour under the power of 350- or 500-horsepower engines. These cranes can reach from 105 to 127 feet maximum with the main booms plus an additional 28 to 103 feet with the boom attachments.

A crane operator for a masonry company sets a box of supplies on a scaffold with the guidance of a worker on top. The crane is a 20-ton Grove truck crane. Foot pedals and mechanical levers are used to run the crane.

A three-axle and a four-axle truck crane are used in tandem to upright this tank for installation at an industrial site. Under the direction of the worker in charge of the installation, the larger crane supports the top, while the smaller tail crane lifts the bottom. The tail crane has a swing-away jib mounted to the side of the boom.

Two truck cranes from Gatwood Crane Rentals are on site to set the main support beams of an airplane hanger. While the 60-ton unit in the distance supports one section of the truss, the 70-ton Grove unit in the foreground is placing the next section along the first, with the assistance of two ironworkers.

All-Terrain Cranes

All-terrain (AT) cranes are the biggest of the mobile hydraulic cranes. They combine the roadability of the truck cranes with the off-road-abilities of the rough-terrain cranes. Some cranes are capable of speeds up to 55 miles per hour. These units also have multiple steering modes and suspension systems to allow for traction both on- and off-road. AT cranes can have as few as two axles or as many as nine. In units with multiple axles, anywhere from two to the total number of axles can have the ability to steer. Capacities range from 22 tons to 1,000 tons. The smaller units have three-section booms while the largest cranes have five- or six-section booms.

A 200-ton crane is the largest that can travel with the boom intact without exceeding weight restrictions for roads. Larger units travel separately from the boom, which is transported on a flatbed trailer. The boom can be attached to the carrier in one of two ways: The first involves an assist crane to lift the boom and hold it in place while it is attached. The other method involves a special trailer that is used to store and transport

Two Lorain 35-ton truck cranes are supporting a large four-section truss for an airplane hanger while the ironworkers begin to bolt it in place. Both cranes worked together to raise the truss until it was in place.

A 70-ton Link-Belt HTC-8670 four-axle hydraulic truck crane is supporting the mast for a highway billboard. A 22-ton Link-Belt ATC-822 hydraulic all-terrain crane is seen behind the HTC-8670.

47

A Lorain 35-ton truck crane is working at a job site placing concrete forms for the building's basement. Since the forms are relatively lightweight, the crane is rigged with a headache ball instead of the sheave block, which rests on the crane's bed. The operator's control cab is visible, showing the electronic display that measures the load and angle for safety. The operator has opened the ceiling hatch for better visibility while watching for overhead obstacles at this very active construction site.

the boom. Called a boom-launching trailer, a hydraulic mechanism slowly pushes the boom into place on the carrier, where it is then attached.

Depending on the lifting capacity of the crane, the overall weight of the crane, or the particular picking requirements for each job, the counterweights used on these AT cranes vary. While the smaller cranes can travel on the road with counterweights on the carrier, the larger units are too heavy and the counterweights must be transported on a separate truck. The counterweights for these cranes consist of several pieces of varying weights and shapes. They stack on the rear of the crane cab and can range from a fixed 3-ton weight to a combination of weights totaling in excess of 70 tons.

Demag offers 11 mobile telescoping cranes. These models range in capacity from 25 to 650 tons. The first two models, which are the smallest, differ from the rest of the units. These two have a single cab for the operator to use for the operation of the crane functions as well as driving the vehicle. These have integrated, nonremovable counterweights and are built on two- and three-axle chassis respectively. With different superstructure configurations, the lifting heights of the larger cranes can be significantly extended beyond their basic capabilities. The largest cranes also have cab options that include beds and night heaters.

The 50-ton capacity AC 50 is the first unit with non-integrated counterweights, side-folding jibs, and a truck carrier with a separate cab. Cranes beginning with the five-axle, 100-ton capacity AC 100 begin to utilize two engines, one for the truck carrier and the second for the crane operations. As the cranes increase in size, other features are incorporated. Demag's newer "oval-oid" boom design begins with the AC 180 crane. The availability of the Superlift attachments begins with the 300-ton AC 300. An additional 48 tons of counterweights are required for the AC 300 when the Superlift is used. The three units

Since the contractor needed to close all lanes of traffic for each pick, work to remove 40-ton cement bridge beams over an interstate highway had to be done between the hours of 1:00 a.m. and 4:00 a.m. A Demag AC1200 500-ton all-terrain hydraulic truck crane was used for five evenings. The crane with its 24-foot jack span occupied two lanes of traffic in addition to the shoulder. As each pick was prepared, traffic was allowed to flow in one lane. When the contractor was ready to make the pick, all traffic was stopped until the beam was set down on the roadway above the highway.

with the highest capacity, the AC 400, AC 500, and AC 650, ride on truck carriers with seven, eight, and nine axles respectively. These three cranes can accept luffing jib extensions up to 90 meters in length.

There are 10 models in the Grove AT crane lineup. These have capacities from 22 to 300 tons. Boom lengths begin at 70 feet and top out at 197 feet for the GMK6250. Maximum tip heights respectively are 121 feet to 374 feet. Similar to the TC cranes, units with 100-ton capacities and greater have two engines, one for the truck carrier and the second for the crane operations. These range from 335 to 571 horsepower for the truck carriers and 141 to 258 horsepower for the crane motors. As a size comparison, consider that the smallest 22-ton AT is powered by a single 190-horsepower engine, while the 100-, 150-, and 175-ton AT cranes have 141-horsepower engines for the crane operations alone.

The heavy cranes feature larger carriers and additional options. The 210-ton GMK5210 has five axles, all of which can steer, while four are drive axles. The six-section boom has a 197-foot maximum length before attaching a 43- to 72-foot bi-fold jib or a 125-foot lattice extension for a maximum tip height of 321 feet. In comparison, the 300-ton GMK6300B has a six-axle carrier with four drive axles and the ability to steer all axles. The five-section boom also has a 197-foot maximum extension. This crane, though, has a 69- to 200-foot luffing jib attachment that provides a maximum tip height of 371 feet. When performing at capacity, roughly 70 tons of counterweights are required at the rear of the crane module.

Many consider Liebherr's strength to be the AT cranes. The product offerings include 12 models with capacities from 42 tons to the giant 1,000-ton LTM 1800. Maximum boom lengths begin at 97 feet and go to 276 feet for the 625-ton model.

A Grove 875 75-ton hydro crane owned by Anthony Crane Rental, Inc. is setting exterior glass panels on this high-rise in downtown Pittsburgh. The crane is operating with 175 feet of boom including the jib.

A City of Chicago bridge crew assembled a bridge on a barge next to their yard along the Chicago River. A five-axle, five-section Krupp 175-ton all-terrain hydro truck crane and 35-ton Tadano rough-terrain hydro crane work together to steady the bridge sections during construction.

A steel beam is removed from a truck prior to being set in place on this bridge project. The long beam will be set on top of the short sections that are sitting on the ground. Here, the ironworkers will attach the fittings and insert bolts to streamline the installation of each beam.

A five-axle Krupp 120-ton all-terrain crane owned by Stevenson Crane Rentals works with 135 feet of boom to set steel beams for a bridge over a rail line. Four out and down stabilizers support the crane. The feet, or pads, for the outriggers have the ability to rest at an angle to provide stability on uneven surfaces.

Lonnie Cranes of California owns this five-axle Grove all-terrain hydraulic truck crane. Each of the 8x10 axles is capable of steering to maximize the maneuverability of this unit to negotiate placement on the job site. All except the front axle are drive axles.

An 18-ton all-terrain hydro crane assists the crew assembling this 75-ton conventional truck crane. The assist crane picks the rigging and boom sections from the transport trucks and sets them in place for the pinning and reeving. The conventional crane is able to set its own counterweights without the assist crane.

A rough-terrain crane model TR-3403 built by Tadano works to place concrete wall panels into tracks along an interstate highway. When completed, these barrier walls will protect residents who live along the highway from some of the noise from the vehicles driving by.

The 1,000-ton unit has a shorter maximum length of 197 feet. The maximum tip heights range from 146 to 479 feet with jib extensions of 47 to 299 feet. Liebherr AT cranes are available with a variety of boom and jib configurations that incorporate folding jibs, lattice fly jibs, and lattice luffing jibs in addition to the telescopic booms.

These cranes ride on truck carriers that have between two and eight axles. Like the other crane builders, cranes with capacities in excess of 100 tons utilize two motors. Carrier engines have from 278- to 570-horsepower outputs while the cranes utilize 163- to 408-horsepower engines. Liebherr produces the diesel engines that power their carriers and cranes. Perhaps the most popular Liebherr AT crane

used in the United States is the 190-ton model LTM 1160/2. This unit has a five-axle carrier with all-wheel steering and five drive axles. It travels with the six-section boom hanging over the rear of the carrier supported by a two-axle dolly. When the crane is on a job site, the dolly is simply stored out of the way until it is needed. The counterweights are transported on a separate truck to keep the road weight of the vehicle down.

Liebherr developed the "Niveaumatik" suspension system for their mobile cranes. This uses hydro-pneumatic springing and axle-load equalization, which is controlled from the driver's cab, allowing various suspension programs to be selected to handle any driving conditions.

An eight-axle, 500-ton Liebherr model LTM 1400 hydraulic crane is rigged with a 140 foot luffing jib to pick and set concrete panels at a hospital construction site. The panels weigh a maximum of 23,000 pounds.

Among the attributes of this suspension system is the ability to lower the oscillations produced while the crane travels over bridges, which is a major concern for large, heavy vehicles.

Several years ago, Liebherr developed a new boom design. The shape of the cross-section changed with what is called the "oviform" boom. The bottom edges of the boom sections are now greatly rounded instead of the customary simple edge rounding design used on the top edges.

This design provides inherent stability against deflection and torsion, which in turn enables optimal lifting capacities in all boom positions.

Link-Belt currently offers one AT crane model, the ATC-822. This unit has a maximum lifting capacity of 22 tons, and a main boom capable of extending to 70 feet before adding up to an additional 43 feet of lattice jib. The crane sits on a two-axle carrier that is powered by a Cummins 6BTA diesel engine.

CHAPTER 3

TOWER CRANES

Building construction that will have more than 10 stories will generally exceed the abilities of a crawler crane. Tower cranes are required to bring supplies and equipment to each floor as it is being built. Tower cranes are freestanding cranes that extend vertically on a steel tower that rises straight up from the ground. On the top of the tower sits a control house for the operator, a counterweight carrier, and most often a horizontal jib section. A trolley runs in and out along the length of the jib placing the rigging at any point along the jib for lifting or delivering materials and equipment.

Towers are irreplaceable in high-rise construction involving steel and concrete buildings. Towers are also used quite often for bridge construction where they will be anchored alongside the main support columns for the bridge. Tower cranes have received an increasing amount of competition from the newer mobile cranes that have the ability to use long boom sections. These cranes require less ground preparation, which results in shorter rigging times. Additionally, mobile cranes rigged for heavy lifts rent out for less than the big tower cranes.

In 1978 there were few heavy-lift crane options. To meet the demand, the Kroll K-10000, a 240-ton heavy-lift tower, was introduced. Some of these large towers were designed for the construction of nuclear power plants, which is currently on the decline. While the small and medium tower cranes are used in the building industry, these large heavy-lift towers can occasionally be found today in the shipbuilding industry, at oil rig construction sites, and at older industrial job sites instead of crawlers or mobile cranes that are too bulky.

Companies manufacturing towers today are Comedil, Favelle Favco, Liebherr, Linden, Peiner, Potain, and Wolff. Styles differ for towers, including placement of the cab, the rail design of the jib, and the use of overhead struts to

Ironworkers assemble a stationary, freestanding Pecco model SK 180 top climbing tower crane at a job site in downtown Chicago. Due to the limited confines of the site, the tower was built higher than normal to clear adjacent obstacles. This tower is configured with 101 feet of jib and a two-part trolley. It has the capacity to pick 13,800 pounds anywhere along the length of the jib. A 190-ton Liebherr mobile truck crane is being used to lift the tower's jib. This tower crane can be configured with a maximum jib length of 196 feet. Transportation of this crane required nine trucks.

There are several types of tower cranes: the city tower, the self-erecting tower, the luffing tower, and the most common style, the horizontal jib tower crane that is simply referred to as a tower crane.

City tower cranes are used at job sites in small cities and areas where the bigger cranes would be harder to transport and erect. They are smaller overall and are assembled onto a freestanding base that is weighted down with counterweights.

Self-erecting cranes are the smallest of the tower cranes. They are designed for easy transport, assembly, and operation. They have a small base and are mounted on a wheeled carrier that is either a truck carrier or a trailered carrier. The carrier has outriggers to support the crane once it is assembled. This crane has a hydraulic system to erect the tower that is pre-assembled as a single unit. The mast, which consists of three sections, telescopes up and out from the stored position in several articulating maneuvers. When assembled, it has the look of a topless crane missing the tail section with the counterweights.

Luffing Towers

By law, property owners have possession of roughly 20 feet of air space directly above their property. With this in mind, before permits are issued and construction of a tower crane is allowed, a contractor must obtain permission from any building owners surrounding a job site before they can install and operate a crane that will swing over the adjacent buildings. In the event that permission is not received, it may be necessary to install a different type of tower crane on the job site—a luffing tower crane, or a gantry crane. These look like a conventional crawler crane set atop a tower instead of resting on tracks. Unlike a regular tower with a horizontal jib, the luffing tower has a conventional lattice main boom that is supported by a mast and is capable of booming up and down. They can be rigged to avoid overswinging neighboring airspace since, unlike a horizontal tower, the luffing

This tower differs from some models in the placement of the cab. While many towers situate the cab at the turntable, the cab for this tower sits away from the turntable, along the jib.

support the jib. Some towers have a tall main section that extends above the cab, whereas others do not. Towers can be large, long-term structures or more portable designs that arrive on wheels and are self-erecting. The cabs can have no amenities for the operator or perhaps a small kitchenette with a microwave and refrigerator.

Two Liebherr tower cranes are on location at a job site in southern Georgia. A new bridge is being built to replace an existing drawbridge. Each tower is set up at one of the main bridge support columns. The tower in the foreground has been tied off to the bridge support in several places.

A luffing tower with a long main boom is set up to assist with the renovation of the state capitol building in Harrisburg, Pennsylvania.

tower has a short tail swing. Luffing towers are also used at job sites where the proximity of buildings or other obstacles prohibits the swing of a conventional tower crane.

Several of these cranes can be placed on a single job site to provide complete coverage while avoiding obstructions on the site or involving neighboring properties. Luffing towers can handle greater capacities than horizontal towers since they can be rigged with heavy-lift attachments. Depending on the design of these cranes, they can be constructed on conventional tower bases that climb, or they rest on a fixed-height

Jake's Crane Service, based in Las Vegas, rents high-powered gantry-type luffing tower cranes instead of the more common horizontal jib styles. They have 11 1970s-vintage Link-Belt TG1900 cranes that were re-manufactured for them. These cranes are faster than the conventional tower cranes and can lift a maximum of 115 or 230 tons depending on the model. Similar to horizontal climbing towers, these cranes are top climbers, that will grow with the project. This crane is being assembled in Chicago with a Liebherr 190-ton assist crane.

tower that cannot be adjusted once the cab and jib are set.

Horizontal Jib Tower Cranes

The basic tower crane is visible in any city across America hovering over construction sites. These units have capacities between 30 and 1,800 metric tons with the ability to reach distances out to 265 feet. Most of these are top slewing cranes, which have a vertical extension, called a roost, that extends over the tower and rises above the horizontal jib. The support cables, which are called the pendant lines, run from the rear of the tail section, over the roost, to support the jib. The tower can be installed on a fixed foundation or on a rail-travelling undercarriage. It can be equipped for either top climbing or bottom climbing configurations.

Climbing refers to the process of raising a tower as the project grows. In the case of a high-rise building, the tower grows as more floors are added to the building. A top climber is easily spotted by the platform extension that surrounds the tower at a point under the turntable. In order for a top climber to grow, extensions are hydraulically hoisted up the outside of the tower. At the platform, the tower is raised enough to accommodate the extension piece that is then slid into place. This process is repeated as many times as needed until the desired height is reached. A bottom climber receives the extension sections near the base of the tower, generally around ground level.

When towers are placed inside buildings, it has become less and less popular to place them in what will become an elevator shaft. The reasoning is simple: The elevator cannot be installed until the tower has been removed. More common placement is an interior spot that will not interfere with any crucial construction aspects that might delay the job. An interesting consideration that may come as a surprise to someone not familiar with the construction trade is that an internal tower crane does not need to

This Liebherr tower sits several stories above the floor being built. Workers below guide the crane operator via radio with instructions about each pick.

occupy space on the lower floors once the building has achieved enough upper floors. When this point is reached, the crane is braced at a point approximately 8–10 floors from the ground. Then it is jacked up from the ground until it reaches the floor with the added bracing. Once this is accomplished, the opening in the lower floors can be filled, allowing completion of these floors and for the advanced work of each trade. Common practice during the construction of large buildings is for successive work to be done on the lower floors even as the upper floors are initiated. This way, by the time the top floors are poured or framed, many of the lower floors have heating, plumbing, electricity, framing, and even painting completed.

Another type of horizontal jib tower crane is the topless saddle jib crane. This unit has no roost above the jib. It is ideal for airport jobs where low headroom is essential. Although the rigging is slightly different, this tower shares all of the other aspects of the conventional tower.

Installation and Disassembly

The first step when using a tower requires communication between the contractor and the

A crane operator keeps an eye on his load from high above the job site. He gets a half hour of climb time at both ends of the day to allow him to get to the cab and get situated for work.

company that will supply the crane. After determining the appropriate crane for the job, the contractor receives specifications for the base to support the tower. Towers are commonly placed alongside the building itself. Another place for a tower is in what becomes an elevator shaft for the building, or as stated earlier, simply a central location within the building that will need to be filled in at a later time. This way, the tower can provide better reach throughout the job site.

The contractor starts by building a base for the tower. This begins with a hole roughly 6 feet square and 15 feet deep that is rebar reinforced. Four anchor stools or bolts are then installed within the hole. The bolts are approximately six feet long and eight inches in diameter. The hole is filled with concrete and allowed to set.

The base section of the tower is bolted to the anchor stools, which are checked and tightened weekly once the crane is installed. Twenty-foot sections of the tower are raised into position with a hydro assist crane and connected to the base section with steel pins until the initial height is reached. The height, which is often achieved with just two sections, is determined either by where the contractor decides to begin or by the minimum height required for the tower's jib to clear obstacles

The Pecco SK 180 is being erected with four counterweights totaling 25,300 pounds. As shown here, the larger three pieces need to be pulled through the counterweight basket while the fourth piece is set from above.

surrounding the construction site. Possible obstacles include any freestanding structure, usually other buildings.

After the tower's height has been achieved, one or two assist cranes will work to set the operator's house, which is also called the cab. Next, the counterweight carrier is set, followed by the jib. Generally, 181 feet is the maximum length of jib to install in the initial operation. The rigging of the pendant lines and connection of the power source follow this. The final step is to set the counterweights into the rear carrier. Portable electric generators often provide the power for tower cranes.

Tower cranes grow with the structures they are helping to build. As additional floors are added, the tower needs to be raised so the jib remains above the work site. As mentioned earlier, this is accomplished at the ground level for a bottom climber or at the top with a top climber. When raising a bottom climber, the base sections are separated with a hydraulic jack that holds the tower in place while additional sections are added and pinned together.

The maximum freestanding tower is approximately 220 feet tall. Beyond this height, the tower gets anchored to the building in jumps of 100 feet. The entire process occurs in reverse when a job is completed and the crane needs to be torn down.

When the crane is no longer needed, it is ready to be dismantled. When it is too high to be reached from street level, a roof-mounted derrick is used. The tower will hoist the components of the derrick to the roof where it is assembled by the ironworkers. Using the derrick, the tower is taken apart and lowered to the ground in sections. When dismantling of the tower is completed, the derrick is torn down manually and taken down to the ground using a construction elevator.

A topless saddle-jib tower crane works at a downtown Kansas City job site near a hospital. One consideration that may have impacted the selection of this crane over a top slewing tower is the close proximity to the hospital's helipad. Minimizing verticle obstacles near a landing zone is a matter of safety.

A tower crane operator, like all crane operators, earns an hourly wage. In addition to the hours spent operating the crane, the operator gets a half hour's pay for climb time at both ends of the day, plus the standard half hour for lunch. Most of the picks involve radio communications because of the operator's obstructed view of the ground and his distance from the workers securing the loads. Even the rooftop picks and deliveries that the operator can see require radio communications because they are so far apart. Nightly, before the operator leaves the tower, the brake that prevents the crane from rotating is released. This allows the crane to weathervane and swing free as a safety measure when the site is closed.

Tower cranes have capacities ranging from 7 to 10 tons based on the design and the location of the trolley along the jib. As big and overbearing as they seem, they are little more than construction elevators. After all, none of the equipment or materials that they pick is very heavy. Normal operations for a tower crane involve picking steel beams, lumber, tools, concrete forms, or a concrete bucket.

A Liebherr tower crane is being dismantled with the assistance of a Liebherr 180-ton hydro crane. If the tower had been higher than the reach of the hydro, or if there had been no ground-level access for the hydro, the ironworkers would have installed a rooftop derrick to handle the job.

CHAPTER 4

AUXILIARY CRANES AND BOOM TRUCKS

Many different industries use trucks that are equipped with a variety of crane-type appliances. Roofers, refuse collectors, building supply companies, truck and equipment repairers, utility companies, towing companies, outdoor sign companies, and emergency service providers have the need to move and deliver heavy equipment or materials. The most common type, with a telescoping device, is called a boom truck. Other trucks have articulating auxiliary cranes or small supplemental boom arms. The lifting capacity ranges from 3,500 pounds to 76,000 pounds, or 38 tons.

Telescoping Boom Trucks

Boom trucks are the largest of these special trucks and feature a telescoping hydraulic boom, which is similar to the boom used on hydro cranes discussed in chapter 3. Boom trucks are popular because they offer the combination of lifting and long reach, without the expense or overall weight of the hydro cranes. Boom trucks are vital to building material suppliers and roofers who need to place their products onto roofs or upper floors. Generally a boom truck will travel to a job site to meet one or more flatbed supply trucks. At larger job sites, a single boom truck will unload many flatbeds.

The major names building these cranes are Elliott, Manitex, National, RO/Stinger, Simon, Terex, and the newcomer Pioneer. Customers can specify a chassis preference from any of the major commercial companies such as Freightliner, International, Ford, Chevy, or Sterling. Guidelines for each boom type will include specifications for gross vehicle weight, wheelbase, cab to axle length, and ratings for both front and rear axles.

The maximum-capacity ratings for these units are measured at an angle of 80 degrees with the boom arm fully retracted. The maximum lifting must occur in an area that is roughly 5 to 10

Prentice is another company that builds articulating-style boom arms. This unit is mounted to the trailer for this northern Wisconsin log hauler. The A-style outriggers are mounted to the trailer and the boom provides a seat and controls for the operator that are high above the trailer. This placement is vital to the operator enabling him to see the logs on the ground so he can stack them properly on the trailer. The tractor is a 1998 Freightliner Classic.

feet from the center of the truck. Based on the capacity of the unit, each has a steel boom with three, four, five, or six sections that telescope outward. The vertical reach will grow with the lifting capacity of the crane, offering a range of between 48 feet and 168 feet. Smaller booms have three sections, while the larger units have four sections, and the biggest have five or six sections. The greater number of sections provides more reach. Each section overlaps the next, which provides increased stability to eliminate bobbing or flexing when the boom is extended. *Bobbing* refers to the motion encountered with some fully extended booms that resembles a flexed fishing pole bobbing in the water. The greater and tighter the overlap, the better the stability of the boom.

Most boom trucks offer 360 degrees of rotation for the boom, although Pioneer has introduced a line of trucks with 500-degree rotation. A boom with 360-degree rotation cannot go past the center point of the crane's radius. In other words, the operator has 180 degrees of rotation in either direction. If the boom makes a pick off the front of the truck, the boom can rotate completely around to the same position, but has to complete a full circle to get to the other side of the truck. The 500-degree rotation allows the operator to swing the boom 250 degrees left or right of the center point, including completely over the front of the truck, without a front outrigger, and without compromising the stability of the truck. Some models offer endless or continuous rotation. This is achieved by the use of a slip ring, which allows the controlling hydraulic fluids to transfer without a hose. The hose is the restricting element that forces the turntable to have a stopping point in either direction.

The majority of boom sections are steel. Some companies build aluminum or fiberglass units for applications including electric utility work. Steel booms are not allowed when working with live power lines.

This National Model 900 telescoping boom rides on a Ford Louisville chassis and is rated at 22,000 pounds. Here, it makes a delivery of roofing materials. To stabilize the five-section boom at full extension requires the use of a front downrigger, two midship A-style outriggers, plus two rear-mounted H-style or out and down riggers.

A truck with an RO Stinger telescoping boom works to hoist decorative bridge trim sections into place over an interstate highway. This unit has both front and rear A-frame–style outriggers to stabilize the unit while it is working.

A delivery of roofing materials is being made with the use of a National model 900 telescoping boom, which is rated at 22,000 pounds. The truck chassis is a Freightliner FL80. Stabilizing the unit when the five-section boom is at full-extension requires the use of a front downrigger, two midship A-style outriggers, plus two rear-mounted H-style out and down riggers. When stored, the crane rests on the boom support at the rear of the truck bed.

The Truck

Overload sensors to override the crane operator and prevent dangerous lifting are common on newer boom trucks though not required in the industry. A power take-off (PTO)–driven hydraulic pump drives the booms. The pump runs off a PTO port on the transmission. Each truck has a winch with a single line. Industry standards usually dictate 200 to 300 feet of 9/16-inch cable on a planetary winch. The winch can be of single- or tandem-speed design. The tandem-speed winch offers increased speed for working, which is restricted by the weight of the load that is attached. The cable is run across the boom arm to the tip, where it is affixed to a down haul weight with a hook. This keeps tension on the cable to get

the cable down to the load and to keep the cable from kinking and ruining the wrap on the winch drum. The cable and winch are both rated. These factors enter into the lifting capacity of the unit and need to surpass the rating of the boom itself.

As with the larger cranes, a common practice with heavier loads is to use sheave blocks at the tip of the boom and to part the line. "Parting the line" means doubling the cable through the sheave block one or more times to distribute the load and reduce the torque required on the winch. Each redoubling of the cable is considered another parting of the line. The number of times that this is done determines how many parts have been used; thus a six-part line has been wrapped three times.

An operator uses a tractor-mounted National series 500C telescoping boom to offload lumber for a construction project. Controls are mounted on both sides of the truck to facilitate operations. The large A-frame outriggers are in place to secure the tractor when the load swings from one side to the other.

Roofers commonly use telescoping hydraulic boom trucks to place their equipment and supplies onto the roof. A worker is directing the truck's operator while setting materials on the roof. This boom has a pallet fork accessory, which simplifies the transport of a full pallet of supplies from the delivery truck directly to the roof.

Like the larger hydro truck cranes, most boom trucks have an available jib section. The jib can either be straight or feature an offset. The jib acts as an extension of the boom and can be designed as a solid structure, or more commonly, with a lattice framework. The lattice design is lighter and can adjust to several positions including 0 degrees, 15 degrees, or 30 degrees. The 0-degree position is required for storage along the main boom.

The jib can be removed completely from the boom, but when it is used, it swings into place with hinges. The procedure requires the operator to boom out slightly to release the jib from the stored position before swinging it into place. Two pins are set before the cable is unhooked from the tip of the boom and threaded into the jib section. The strength of the jib is limited. Most have a maximum capacity to pick 2,000 pounds down to 500 pounds at the lower angles of elevation.

Boom trucks with sufficient capacities can be fitted with a man basket. Depending on the design, a man basket can hold one, two, or four people, although the two-man basket is most common. The basket will generally be stored on the bed of the boom truck and attaches to the end of the boom with pins. The basket pins are separate from the jib pins, which permits the basket to be pinned to a jib with limits on the allowable extension.

The majority of boom trucks have tandem rear axles, although the smallest units can be built on a single-axle chassis. Most have a truck-mounted appliance located behind the cab with the boom resting over the rear. This is the preferred position since the center of gravity is better for driving and turning with the weight distributed between the truck's axles. Some styles are mounted at the rear with the boom resting over the front of the truck. Rear mounts usually are larger units with greater boom

Sign companies also use nontubular booms, though these are almost always equipped with an aluminum ladder. Here, the worker is using the boom to stabilize the sign while he works off an extension ladder.

lengths that require a different type of weight distribution. These place the heaviest portion over the rear tandem axles.

Another style is called a tractor mount. The boom is mounted behind the cab of a tractor with a fifth wheel that is used to pull trailer loads of equipment or materials. Tractor-mounted booms rest on a support stand that is mounted between the front bumper and the engine.

Each boom truck requires stabilizers to support the unit during lifting operations. Most units use some style of outriggers. Commonly called A-frame outriggers, these are integral to the base of the crane unit and extend out from the truck at an angle until they reach the ground. Depending on the size of the boom, the outriggers vary in thickness and length, with the bigger stabilizers corresponding to the larger cranes. Most of the manufacturers use this design.

Manitex also uses other types of rear stabilizers for certain models. The product line uses an H-style rear stabilizer on the smaller trucks; these are vertical double-acting hydraulic cylinders which extend straight down underneath the truck's bed and are located just behind the rear axle. Some medium-sized models use an A-frame outrigger at the rear that is smaller than the main A-frame support, while the rear stabilizers on heavier Manitex trucks extend out from the truck and down. Jack spread, which is the total width of the vehicle with the outriggers in place, varies from 18 feet to 23 feet. Units manufactured by National beginning with 10-ton capacities also incorporate rear stabilizers. The biggest units replace the A-type outriggers with larger H-style outriggers that extend straight out from the truck with support beams parallel to the ground. At the end of each support jack is a leg that lowers to the ground. Depending on the design and size of the crane, it will either use one set of midship jacks alone or a total of four jacks

A small Auto Crane 15-foot, truck-mounted crane with a 3,500-pound capacity provides the lifting power required by this on-site equipment repair mechanic. Here, part of the crawler assembly for a bulldozer has been lifted out of the way.

The Skyhoist model boom truck is popular with outdoor sign companies. The tubular boom has a telescoping aluminum ladder attached, which allows a worker to reach building-mounted or pole-mounted signs. This unit is also equipped with a man basket that allows a worker a more stable base as compared to working from the ladder.

A city repair crew uses the boom arm from their IMT crane to steady an iron railing while a welder secures it in place. Several workers would be required to assist the welder without the use of the boom. Apparently, the other workers were sent along in case they were needed.

with the third and fourth located at the rear of the truck's body. Some manufacturers require the addition of a front down rigger to stabilize the unit while working over the front. This is generally applicable with a rear-mounted boom.

Differing from the other companies, Pioneer has developed a system of outriggers that have an X pattern. Located midship at the base of the crane unit, these outriggers fold up and drop in a straight line. They are built at an angle to the truck's frame, but not the industry-standard 90-degree angle. When deployed, they articulate

down and telescope outward. The angle minimizes the total jack spread while offering increased stability. This in turn allows for more rotation than other designs. All four models in the Pioneer line utilize the same outrigger design with a jack spread of 17 feet 10 inches.

Each stabilization design can level the unit. When in the ideal position, the truck's wheels should rest on the ground; otherwise the unit can teeter with the terrain or with shifts in the balance of the load. Dual operator controls are positioned at the base of the boom structure, on

Cranes built by Pioneer utilize a unique design for the outriggers. The four legs hinge downward to the ground at an angle other than 90 degrees from the truck's frame. This provides the operator with a 500-degree rotation that allows for swinging past the midpoint on either side of the vehicle. This also permits the handling of loads over the front of the truck without the need for a front stabilizer. This unit is built on a Freightliner FL112 chassis.

Three building material delivery trucks loaded with drywall were dispatched to this job site. Two have knuckle-boom cranes to hoist the supplies several floors off the ground; each has an elevated seat for the operator and both are equipped with the pallet-fork attachment to lift the stacks of drywall.

either side. This allows the operator to manipulate the boom to work off either side of the truck with a clear line of sight. Smaller- and most medium-sized units feature an exterior control panel that consists of several levers. The operator stands on the bed of the truck and maneuvers the outriggers for setup and the boom for lifting.

National, one of the largest companies producing boom trucks, features a product line with 10 models that have 5 ton up to 36 ton capacities. The first eight models feature midship designs with exterior controls for the operator. The two

units that round out the product mix are rear-mounted designs that differ from the midship models. These units feature an enclosed cab for the operator. Unlike the exterior controls that require an operator to stand, the enclosed control cab offers a seated position that rotates with the boom similar to the all-terrain hydro truck cranes. National booms are painted white and have a small brown and black stripe before the National name.

Pioneer has four base models to choose from. These range from 15 tons up to 28.8 tons of lifting

This Swedish-made Hiab knuckle-boom articulating crane is mounted to a Ford F800 series chassis with a flatbed. Workers are using the crane to load rolls of chain link fence onto the truck's bed.

capacity. They offer three- and four-section steel boom construction. The top-of-the-line model is available with a rotating control center providing a seated and enclosed work area for the operator. Unlike National's, Pioneer's enclosed operator model is a midship design. The booms are white with distinctive short blue and red stripes.

Manitex has 12 standard behind-the-cab models and 6 rear-mount models in their "S" series. The standard models have capacities ranging from 9 tons to 30 tons and the "S" series ranges from 21 tons to 38 tons. These have three- and four-section booms. All of the "S" series units have a turret-mounted operator control station with a seat. Manitex boom trucks are easy to spot because the booms are painted dark blue.

Elliott builds trucks for construction and maintenance applications. They have fully hydraulic cranes and work platforms. Their cranes have capacities up to 15 tons with the ability to reach from 35 to 140 feet. They offer rear-mount or mid-mount styles.

Boom trucks can be equipped with several attachments for specialized work. By employing these various accessories, boom trucks can be used to perform an array of jobs that would otherwise require several specialized vehicles. A pallet fork can be attached to the boom tip and used to load and unload building materials that are transported on wooden pallets. Whereas a forklift can place the materials at street level, the pallet fork attachment allows for the placement of supplies onto upper floors of a building without having to remove them from the pallet. A clamshell bucket allows for the movement of loose materials most often associated with removing fill from a hole or refilling a hole upon completion of a job.

Utility companies will often accessorize boom trucks with augers to drill holes for the placement of utility poles with diameters from 12 to 36 inches. These are generally supplemented with a hydraulically operated pole grab accessory to place the utility pole into the new hole. Outdoor sign companies utilize the same attachments to install freestanding pole signs.

One manufacturer that specializes in lighter-weight service trucks is the Phoenix Corporation. They build the Skyhoist, Skyhook, and Sponco models. The Skyhoist is a combination aerial service platform unit and crane with a maximum capacity of 8,700 pounds and a top working height of 92 feet. The Skyhook is an aerial crane with a tubular boom, and the Sponco is a lightweight aerial ladder.

Though most boom trucks have a heavier square steel boom design, it is not uncommon among outdoor sign companies to find lighter-weight tubular booms, such as the Skyhook. These can be equipped with a lightweight aluminum ladder attached to the boom that telescopes with the boom so a worker can climb to the end. Many of these designs also incorporate a lightweight man basket at the tip. Sign companies use these for elevating a worker to reach outdoor signs to handle basic maintenance such as bulb replacement and cleaning in addition to the wiring of new installations. They also use the booms to raise signs or poles for installation. Since most signs are fairly lightweight in design, these companies do not require the heavier boom trucks for the majority of their duties. More often than not, though, at least one of the boom trucks will augment the fleet of a large sign company for the heavier jobs.

The smallest telescopic booms built by companies such as Auto Crane and IMT are auxiliary-mounted compact cranes for utility trucks that are used to assist with lightweight lifting. Trucks utilizing these devices are not considered boom trucks, but generally assist mechanics who provide on-site service for trucks and construction equipment. These individuals may need to repair tracks on a crawler device or other heavy mechanical components that cannot be lifted easily by one person. The booms allow the mechanics to work with parts that otherwise would require the help of several other people.

Utility workers in Sac City, Iowa, set a utility pole with their new boom truck. The pole is held by the boom with a pole grab accessory. This truck is also equipped with a digger derrick and one-person man basket. In addition, it has the ability to carry poles to a job site. It is built on a Freightliner FL80 4x4 chassis with a Pitman Polecat #M50-plus boom. The control seat for the operator is elevated, which allows an unobstructed view of the work. The boom is rigged with nylon rope instead of wire rope due to the proximity of live wires on job sites.

Articulating Auxiliary Cranes

Material handling that does not require the reach offered by boom trucks is often handled by the more compact articulating booms. Where a telescoping boom can extend to lengths up to 170 feet, the largest articulating booms, also called hydraulic knuckle-boom cranes, reach up to 70 feet. Most often, these designs are found making street-level job site deliveries of building materials. For example, refuse collection companies use small articulating booms for the pickup and delivery of garbage dumpsters, and road construction suppliers use these units to deliver sewer pipe. Another common use for an articulating boom is for the delivery of large tires used for off-road heavy-duty construction equipment. National, Hiab, Prentice, and Palfinger are four of the largest companies producing these cranes. Crane capacities range from as little as 1 ton to upwards of 20 tons for the largest models. Mounting varies from behind the cab of the truck to the rear of the truck's bed. Like the boom trucks, the articulating cranes require stabilizers and are offered with either A-type angled outriggers or the heavier H-style out and down jacks, depending on the size of the crane. Smaller units have midship stabilizers only, while the heavier cranes require the addition of rear outriggers for added support.

Several accessory attachments are available to enhance the capabilities of the articulating cranes similar to the telescoping cranes. Clamshell buckets, augers, man baskets, pallet forks, timber grapplers, pole grabs, jibs, brick pack grapples, and orange peel grabs are some of the general and specialized attachments. While the use of most of these accessories was described during the telescoping boom section, several others are mentioned here.

The timber grapple is a claw-like device that is designed for loading large timber on and off a flatbed truck for the logging industry. This is generally accompanied by an elevated work platform with a seat for the operator. The higher vantage point offers the necessary overall view of the stack of timber on the ground and is vital to the proper loading of the logs onto the truck.

A brick pack grapple is designed to secure a load of bricks that are conventionally packaged in a uniform manner. This grabs the stack on two sides with special skids. The orange peel grab has several individually controlled curved pieces that come to a point at the ends. Most often, this is used like an enormous claw for grabbing scrap or recyclable materials in a yard.

Hiab and Palfinger cranes imported into the United States are generally the smaller and midrange styles. Hiab is produced in Sweden and Palfinger in Austria. Subsequently, the popularity and usage of their larger units are most heavily concentrated in Europe where these designs dominate a market that is held by the telescoping boom trucks in the United States.

European fire brigades, for example, commonly incorporate a Palfinger crane onto their specialized rescue vehicles to lift cars and trucks at accident sites. The knuckle-boom crane is mounted to the rear of the vehicle. Fire departments in the United States generally use specialized lifting tools or solicit the assistance of a towing company.

Several specialized uses for some of the cranes introduced in this chapter are highlighted in the next chapter.

This flatbed truck was outfitted with an 1,150-kilogram articulating boom. This allows one worker to deliver or pick up refuse dumpsters from customer locations. Small outriggers are all that are required to stabilize this truck.

CHAPTER 5

SPECIAL APPLICATION CRANES

Cranes are used in a multitude of applications besides those described in the previous chapters. Dock work, emergency services, towing, scrap collection, and railroad work are a few examples of fields where cranes are used in either unexpected ways or with different apparatus than what is used in more common applications. As a matter of fact, all cranes are not mobile.

Stationary Cranes

Many cranes are stationary and work inside factories and warehouses. These overhead cranes are mounted on steel rails that usually span the length of a building. This allows an operator with a hard-wired remote control to travel the crane from one end of the facility to the other for lifting heavy objects and moving them within the building.

Another type of stationary crane is a lattice boom crane mounted to a pedestal. Often found dockside to load and offload ships, these cranes are set on a high perch to allow the operator to look down on the ship and cargo holds. These are the same cranes that are found elsewhere riding on crawler tracks, and they therefore have the capacity to lift heavy loads. They differ, however, from stationary tower cranes that offer a high vantage point for the operator with excellent reach but minimal lifting capacities. Sand, coal, ore, and other heavy raw materials are shipped on barges and need to be offloaded for storage into materials yards. The crane will use a clamshell bucket to scoop the product from the

The Lutherville, Maryland, Fire Department demonstrates the use of the crane mounted to their heavy rescue unit. The crane keeps the car from moving so the firefighters can perform the extrication to free victims trapped inside. The 8,000-pound capacity crane is mounted to a rescue squad that was built by Saulsbury Fire Apparatus on a Mack MC chassis.

A stationary crane along the Chicago River is used to place sailboats into the water each spring and to remove them to dry-dock each fall. The crane has a capacity of 19 tons.

Two Lampson LTL-2600 Transi-Lift cranes complete a world-record lift for two land base mobile lift cranes. They are shown lifting a 1,297-ton topside module onto a concrete gravity offshore oil platform in Australia. The pick required over a 60-meter height at a 56-meter radius. Both cranes were configured with 460 feet of main boom and rigged with 32 parts of 1 1/2 inch load line. *Lampson International Ltd.*

The emergency services division of the New York Police Department operates three Jumper Response Vehicles. Each identical unit carries large fans to inflate giant air bags that are designed to cushion the fall of an individual who leaps from a building. Two different bag styles are capable of catching a jumper from a building up to 10 stories tall or 20 stories tall respectively. These units also respond to water rescue calls. They carry a rigid-hull inflatable boat that rests above the truck's body. An Auto Crane 3,500-pound boom arm is mounted on the truck to assist officers in retrieving the boat and replacing it again.

barge, lift it up, and swing with it until it can be discharged onto a pile, into a truck, or onto a conveyer belt that will carry it to a yard away from the dock.

An unusual fixed-position crane resides along the Chicago River in a boat yard. It is used to load and unload sailboats from the boatyard and the river. This crane features a lattice- type boom that rests on a turntable near the edge of the river. The operator sits in a small sheltered work area roughly 50 feet from the main boom and uses a mechanical gear system to engage the winch and boom movements.

Emergency Services

Telescoping booms and articulating booms with medium capacities can be found in many applications outside of construction, material delivery and handling, utility work, and sign installation, as mentioned previously. One example can be found with the New York City police and fire departments. They both use the smallest available boom arms on special deployment vehicles that each department runs. Both departments carry rigid-hull inflatable boats for rescue work. The boats are mounted on the top of a rescue vehicle alongside an Auto Crane

This crane travels on a set of rails along the river where barges bring loads of raw materials for the production of concrete. The crane has a clamshell bucket and scoops piles of raw materials before dropping them into a hopper. The hopper deposits the material onto a conveyor belt that routes the product to a pile elsewhere in the yard. A steel bar connecting the crane and the hopper allows them both to move when the operator chooses while maintaining the appropriate spacing between them.

3,500-pound telescoping boom arm. The boom is used to remove the boat for use and replace it afterward. There are a total of five units in service in New York City with these booms.

Following the lead of European fire services, a small number of fire departments throughout the United States have mounted larger booms onto their heavy-duty rescue trucks to assist with vehicle accidents and below-ground rescue work. Fire departments in Lutherville and Aberdeen, Maryland; Oakland, California; Phoenix, Arizona; Nutley, New Jersey; and York Township, Pennsylvania, all have cranes mounted to their rescue squads. These cranes provide added flexibility when performing intricate rescues.

Used in conjunction with the other specialized tools and equipment that they carry, the cranes provide the ability to lift objects higher than would be possible with air bags or jacks that lift from underneath. The cranes also allow these departments to control all aspects of a rescue when overhead lifting or support is required, whereas they might otherwise need to employ the services of an outside agency.

Special Crawlers

A magnet is an accessory that is fitted to a lattice boom crane for use in scrapyards. Material is dumped on the ground by trucks, and then bulldozers or front-end loaders will assist with moving the scrap if needed to a position within the crane's reach. The giant magnet on the end then grabs the scrap and the crane swings around to place the material onto a belt or directly into a giant compactor.

Standard lattice boom crawler cranes can also be found with rail attachments for work along the railroad tracks. Sometimes the crane is mounted to a flat car and pulled by a locomotive instead of travelling under its own power. Various attachments can be used including a

A crawler crane with a magnet attached to the boom works in a scrapyard to keep up with the arriving scrap metal. Both large and small trucks line up to dump their loads. The scrap is dropped into the compactor unit where it develops a whole new look.

clamshell bucket for grabbing railroad ties or gravel for the track bed. Large rail-mounted cranes are also used to pick up derailed train cars at accident sites in remote areas that are only accessible via rail.

Towing

The heavy-duty wreckers used by towing companies are also considered cranes. These large telescoping booms have capacities ranging from 35 tons to 70 tons. Unlike cranes, heavy wreckers have the ability to both winch and lift. Wreckers need to winch vehicles that are off the road, in water, mud, snow, or any other situation that would prevent a vehicle from travelling under its own power. Towing companies also have heavy wreckers called rotators that can swing from side to side for a better working vantage in addition to being able to swing with a load attached. These cranes have limits on the distances they are capable of reaching as compared to the booms used on conventional cranes and boom trucks.

Mega Cranes

The major crane manufacturers mentioned throughout this book build cranes of all sizes. Generally the top-of-the-line crane, though, will be one with a reasonably large buyers' market to enable the company to recoup its costs and make a profit. There are always special projects that exist which require longer reaches or heavier lifts than the commercial cranes can handle. Though some of these tasks can be accomplished with special rigging or the use of multiple cranes working together, other jobs need to be handled by custom-built cranes that barely resemble anything that has yet been illustrated in this book.

In the towing industry, the rotator is generally considered the biggest crane available. Here, a 60-ton Century rotator has picked a car out of a ditch and is placing it on a 30-foot Chevron carrier for the trip to the yard. The rotator and the carrier both have a Freightliner Classic chassis.

This flat-car–mounted lattice boom crane is fitted with a clamshell bucket. It is travelling down a section of track that is in need of new railroad ties. The train stops every 100 or so feet and the crane grabs a load of ties from the flat car and drops them along the right of way.

Transi-Lift

One of the companies that responds to these calls worldwide is Neil F. Lampson, Inc. They have equipment to transport the heaviest loads and the heavy rigging to make the biggest picks and provide the longest reach. Although they have many conventional cranes, the largest cranes in Lampson's fleet are the Lampson Transi-Lift (LTL) series. There are four different Transi-Lift series cranes; each is distinguishable by slightly different body designs and lifting capacities. These cranes were developed in response to the growing needs for specialized heavy lifts and rigging. They are mobile crawler cranes that are customized to the specific lift requirements of each job. Like any crane, they can be transported in pieces to a job site anywhere in the world. A Transi-Lift is also mobile while on site, which allows it to be assembled in one spot before crawling into place for the pick or picks.

Construction of the Miller Stadium in Milwaukee County, Wisconsin, came to a swift halt after a catastrophic accident caused a unique crane to fail. The load, a 400-ton section of the retractable domed roof, came crashing down on another crane, killing three ironworkers who were suspended in a man basket. A view of the scene after the accident shows the magnitude of the collapse and of the entire job site. This image shows at least six cranes on the site, one hydro and five crawlers with a variety of attachments and configurations. There were six other crawler cranes around the site in addition to the one that was destroyed.

THE ROLES OF RECOVERY CRANES

A fully loaded tractor-trailer combination ran into a drainage ditch and rolled onto its side along a highway in Illinois. Ernie's crane made the pick with two heavy wrecker assist cranes at the front and rear of the disabled semi. The front unit was used to winch the semi once it was uprighted.

Another aspect of the towing industry involves the use of conventional boom trucks, rough-terrain, or all-terrain hydro cranes. Many duties in recovery work require that a towing company have access to a hydro crane for specialized lifting or the off-road capabilities of a rough-terrain unit. Some companies rent a crane if needed whereas others have chosen to own their own. Until recently, Ernie's Wrecker Service in Illinois owned one of the most impressive cranes in the towing industry. It was a rear-mounted National series 1500 36-ton crane on a Peterbilt 359 custom chassis with an enclosed operator's cab. Painted in the classic style of the towing industry to match the balance of the fleet, the crane had chrome wheels, tow-style body compartments, emergency warning lights, and reflective lettering. This unit turned heads whenever it drove down the road.

Although the crane had far superior reach and lifting ability than a heavy wrecker, all it could do is lift. While it was a beautiful rig and performed well on several recoveries, one of the downfalls of the crane was that it could not winch or tow. Winching, as mentioned earlier, is paramount in the towing industry. After the crane went to work performing a recovery, a second rig was needed to tow the recovered vehicle. In addition, the operator needed to remain in the crane's cab during a recovery. A wrecker, on the other hand, has controls at the rear of the truck that allow the operator to constantly check the chains and straps as the recovery takes place. As often as necessary, the operator can stop and simply walk to check rigging and the progress of the work.

One other detrimental aspect of the crane for a company that does not specialize in crane work is the need for specially trained assistants to direct the operator and handle the rigging, whereas anyone can help an operator pull cables from a heavy wrecker or rotator. Due to the fancy and top-of-the-line design of this particular crane, finding a buyer in the crane industry proved difficult. Basically, the truck was too nice for most operators.

If the capacity of one LTL is not sufficient to accomplish a pick, two Transi-Lifts can be use together to double the capacity.

These cranes are available for sale or rent. At the time of this writing, Lampson is believed to have four of these units in service worldwide handling jobs in the United States and helping to make preparations for the Olympic games in Australia. There are another six or so that have been produced and sold to other companies.

The Transi-Lift has been engineered to lift up to 1,500 tons, although a model with a 3,000-ton capacity is said to be in the works. The lift itself represents only part of the project when the LTL is used. The ability to achieve height and reach while lifting these heavy loads is where these specialized cranes perform especially well. Picking 771 tons with 340 feet of boom or putting a 600-ton dome cover at an electric powerplant while working at a 140-foot radius are examples of the Transi-Lift at work. These massive cranes have seats for three operators who work together controlling different sections of the crane. One handles the main boom functions while the other two have the task of maneuvering the crawlers. Depending on the job requirements, a Transi-Lift can be configured with over 1,400 tons of counterweights.

Mammoet

Mammoet, International is another company that specializes in heavy lifts and the transportation of heavy loads. They have jacks, special transport units, and their own ships and barges to move the heaviest loads within a job site or to points around the world. The bulk of this work is for the nuclear energy, chemical, and petroleum industries.

Their fleet of heavy-lift cranes includes the capacity to lift up to 1,750 tons with crawler cranes and 1,200 tons with lattice boom mobile cranes using Superlift attachments. Mammoet's newest crane is the MGS-50, which recently

completed its first North American picks by setting vessels at refineries in Texas. Set up with a ring-type base section, it set four 730-ton columns at one site followed by three additional vessels of 311 tons, 512 tons, and 726 tons at radii of 316 and 224 feet. The MGS-50 was rigged with roughly 234 feet of main boom, 142 feet of jib, and 2,500 tons of counterweights.

Van Suemeren

The king of international heavy lift is Van Suemeren Holland BV. They are a market leader in the horizontal and vertical transports working both onshore and offshore. The company has more than 200 lattice boom cranes in several styles in its fleet. They claim to be the only company owning five Demag CC 4800 crawler cranes capable of lifting 1,600 tons when fitted with the Superlift attachments. Van Seumeren also owns a 1,600-ton Demag CC 12600. This is the world's largest crane and when configured with a ring base, the capacity increases to 2,000 tons. Their truck cranes have capacities up to 1,000 tons with Superlift attachments and the largest hydraulic crane, a Liebherr LTM 1800, has an 800-ton capacity.

The 2,000-ton capacity Platform Twin Ring is the newest heavy-lift crane the company uses. The crane's most interesting design feature is its mobility—it can be broken down into standard 20-foot shipping containers. Van Suemeren is adding five of these units to its fleet.

They also maintain a fleet of offshore equipment that includes tugboats and 250- and 300-metric-ton-capacity barge-mounted cranes. The new generation heavy-lift crane, the Rambiz, is the largest water-based vessel. This is a twin-hull, catamaran-style lifting vessel, which is actually two lift barges linked by a connector beam. In other words, it is an oceangoing pontoon vessel. Cranes on each of the barge platforms have a 2,000-ton capacity each. If the need arises, the Rambiz can be separated into two 2,000-ton lifting barges.

INDEX

Aberdeen, Maryland, Fire Department, 87
All-terrain cranes, 47, 48, 51, 54, 55
American, 11, 21, 31, 32
    Pedestal cranes, 21
    Tower attachments, 21
Anthony Crane Rental, Inc., 22, 42, 51
Articulating booms, 87
Assist crane, 29
Augers, 83
Auto Crane, 80, 87
Auxiliary cranes, 83
Boom trucks, 70, 72, 75, 76, 78, 80
Boom, 14, 15
Boom-launching trailer, 48
Brick pack grapples, 83
Broderson, 38
Caisson drilling attachment, 7
Capacities
    Conventional domestic crawler
        cranes, 16
    Crawler cranes, 18
    German crawler cranes, 16
Car body, 12
Central Crane Company, 37
Chellino Crane Service, 27
Chevron, 91
Chevy, 67
City tower cranes, 58
Clamshell bucket, 25, 83, 85, 92
Comedil, 57
Crane
    Assembly, 26, 28
    Parts of, 11–16
Crawlers, On-site job duties, 29
Demag, 11, 26, 31, 32, 37, 48, 51
    Superlift, 32
Derrick booms, 32
Dielco, 20
Drill rig attachment, 16
Elliott, 67, 80
Emergency Services, 87, 88
Ernie's Wrecker Service, 94
Favelle Favco, 57
Fixed fly jib, 32
Fly section, 45
Folding jibs, 54
Ford, 67
Freightliner Classic, 67
Freightliner, 67
Gatwood Crane Rentals, 46
Grove, 31, 32, 37, 38
    AT crane, 51
    T cranes, 41
    Truck cranes, 45
Headache ball, 48
Hiab, 79, 83
Horizontal jib tower cranes, 60, 61
Housing, 12
Hydro truck cranes, 31, 35, 37
IMT, 80

Industrial cranes, 37, 38
International, 67
Jake's Crane Service, 60
Jib section, 14
Jib, 15, 45, 72, 83
Kobelco, 11
Krupp, 37
Lampson Transi-Lift (LTL) series, 91
Lattice boom, 32
Lattice fly jibs, 54
Lattice jib, 55
Lattice luffing jibs, 54
Liebherr, 11, 21, 22, 31, 32, 37, 51,
    54, 55, 57, 61
    AT cranes, 54
Lifting capacities, 18
Lima, 11, 31, 32
Linden, 57
Link-Belt, 11, 21, 22, 31, 32, 37
    RT cranes, 41
    Truck cranes, 45
Little Giant, 37
Load line, 14
Lonnie Cranes of California, 53
Lorain, 37
Luffing crane, 69
Luffing jib, 12, 16, 29, 32
Luffing towers, 58–60
Lutherville, Maryland, Fire Department,
    85, 87
Main strut, 16
Mammoet, 95
Man basket, 83, 93
Manitex, 67, 75, 80
Manitowoc, 11, 21–26, 31, 32, 35
    MAX-ER, 24
    Ringer, 25, 26
Mast, 12
Maxer attachment, 11, 20
Mega cranes, 91
Miller Stadium, 93
Modern crane market, 21–26
National, 67, 75, 78, 83
Nationwide Erectors, 9
Neil F. Lampson, Inc., 91
New York Police Department, Jumper
    Response Vehicles, 86
Nutley, New Jersey, Fire Department, 87
Oakland, California, Fire Department, 87
Oiler, 16
Operator, Duties, 16
Orange peel grabs, 83
Oviform boom, 55
P&H, 31, 37
Palfinger, 83
Pallet forks, 83
Peiner, 57
Pendant lines, 12
Phoenix Corporation, 80
Phoenix, Arizona, Fire Department, 87

Pick, Calculating, 18, 21
Pile driver, 16
Pioneer, 69, 76–78
Pole grabs, 83
Potain, 57
Prentice, 67, 83
Primary crane, 29
Recovery cranes, 94
Ring horse crane, 21
Ring-type attachments, 29
RO/Stinger, 67
Rough-terrain cranes, 38, 41
Saulsbury Fire Apparatus, 85
Secondary crane, 29
Self-erecting cranes, 58
Series-2, 11
Sheave block, 14, 48, 70
Shuttlelift, 38
Simon, 67
Sky horse crane, 21
Skyhoist, 80
Skyhook, 80
Special crawlers, 88
Sponco, 80
Stationary cranes, 85, 87
Steel boom, 80
Sterling, 67
Stevenson Crane Rentals, 52
Tadano, 37
    RT cranes, 41
Tail crane, 29, 45
Telescopic booms, 54, 87
Telescoping boom trucks, 67, 69
Terex, 67
Timber grapplers, 83
Topless saddle jib crane, 61, 65
Tower attachment, 18, 24, 29
Tower crane, 21
    Installation and disassembly,
        61–63, 65
Towing, 88, 91
Transi-Lift, 91, 92, 95
Transporting, Crawler cranes, 18
Truck-mounted cranes, 41, 45
Tubular boom, 80
Van Suemeren, 95
Whip line, 14
Wolff, 57
Work horse crane, 21
Wrecking ball, 15
York Township, Pennsylvania, Fire
    Department, 87

Models
American
    11020, 21
    1320, 21
    Crawler crane, 15
    229, 21
Auto Crane

Boom arm, 86
    Truck-mounted crane, 75
Century rotator, 91
Demag
    AC 100, 48
    AC 180, 48
    AC 300, 48
    AC 400, 51
    AC 50, 48
    AC 500, 51
    AC 650, 51
    AC1200 all-terrain hydraulic truck, 49
    CC12600, 26, 95
    CC1800, 26
    CC2500, 26
    CC2800, 26
    CC4800, 26, 95
    CC6400, 26
    CC8200, 26
    Ringlift, 27
Ford F800 series, 79
Freightliner
    Classic, 91
    FL112, 77
    FL80, 70, 81
Grove
    875 hydro crane, 51
    All-terrain hydraulic truck crane, 53
    Crawler, 14
    GMK5210, 51
    GMK6250, 51
    GMK6300B, 51
    RT880 rough-terrain crane, 38
    Truck crane, 42, 46
IMT crane, 76
Kroll K10000, 57
Krupp
    All-terrain crane, 52
    All-terrain hydro truck crane, 51
Liebherr
    Assist crane, 60
    Hydraulic crane, 69
    Hydro crane, 65
    LG 1550, 32
    LR 11200, 21
    LR 1250, 21
    LR 1400, 21
    LR 1550, 21, 23
    LR 1650, 21
    LR 1800, 21
    LTM 1160 all-terrain hydro truck
crane, 38
    LTM 1160/2, 54
    LTM 1400 hydraulic crane, 55
    LTM 1800, 95
    LTR 1800, 22
    Mobile truck crane, 57
    Tower cranes, 59
Lima
    700 TC conventional truck crane, 31

Conventional truck crane, 9
Link-Belt
    ATC-822, 55
    HC-238H, 32
    HC-248H, 32
    HC-278H, 32
    HTC-8670 hydraulic truck crane, 47
    LS-138, 18
    LS-138H, 16, 22
    LS-208H, 22
    LS-218H, 22
    LS-238H, 22
    LS-248H, 22
    LS-278H, 22
    TG1900 crane, 60
    Truck crane, 35
Lorain
    Conventional truck crane, 33
    LRT434, 41
    Truck crane, 47, 48
Mack MC, 85
Mammoet MGS-50, 95
Manitowoc
    111, 24
    21000, 18, 24, 28
    222, 24
    2250, 24
    3900, 15, 18, 22
    3900T Vicon series lattice boom
        truck, 8
    3950, 22
    4100, 22, 24
    4600, 22
    777, 18, 24
    777 Epic series crane, 12
    777T, 32, 35
    888, 18, 22, 24, 27
    M 1200 ringer assembly, 26
    M-250, 11, 26
    M-250T, 32, 37
    Epic Series, 22, 24
    Vicon Series, 22
National
    1500 crane, 94
    500C telescoping boom, 71
    900 telescoping boom, 70
P&H rough-terrain crane, 42
Pecco SK 180, 57, 63
Peterbilt 359, 94
Pitman Polecat #M50-plus boom, 81
RO/Stinger telescoping boom, 69
Skyhoist model boom, 75
Tadano
    Rough-terrain hydro crane, 51
    TR-3403 rough-terrain crane, 54
Van Suemeren
    Platform Twin Ring, 95
    Rambiz, 95